FREIGHTERS AND PILGRIMS

Two stories of Western Immigration in 1865

Dangers of the Trail in 1865

By Charles E. Young

and

Days on the Road

Sarah Raymond Herndon

2022, Knowledge Keepers Bookstore

ISBN: 978-1-7377062-2-9

Contents

Since this book is a true diary, there are no chapters.

Introduction

The two stories told in this volume took place during the summer of 1865, and nearly along the same route from Missouri to the West.

The first book, Dangers of the Trail in 1865 is the biographical narrative of 19-year-old Charles Young, who followed Horace Greely's advice to "go west young man, and grow up with the country." Young, along with two friends, left New York near the end of the Civil War in July 1865, bound for Colorado. He traveled west as a cook with a freight team.

It is from his narrative that I took the title for this book:

> We were not long in finding a suitable camping spot a mile from the town and the same distance from the many corrals of the great Western *freighters and pilgrims*, as the immigrants were called.

The second book in this volume is Days on the Road, the diary of Sarah Raymond on her trip overland from Missouri to Montana. Her account was written each night on the trail, and later published in The Husbandman, a local newspaper.

As I researched these two stories, I found that both Charles and Sarah traveled roughly the same route much of the way to Colorado, experienced some of the same river crossings, and heard the same tales of Indian massacres.

While both stories are similar in many ways, there are some stark difference: Sarah's journey was with families moving west to settle, and was fairly safe and pleasant; Charles experienced a more dangerous journey with a group of all male freighters and the rough atmosphere of the mining towns. There are some interesting comparisons to be made.

If you've read *True Stories of Nebraska Pioneers* or *Up the Western Trail*, two other books in this series, you'll notice how Nebraska played a very important part of the western migration. The plains, the Platte River, the Indians… thousands of pioneers, cowboys, Indians, trappers, miners, and other characters of the Western story had their time in the wilds of Nebraska.

Speaking of the Indians, both writers shared similar views of the natives of the Plains. Their opinions will shock some readers today, but history is best read just as it happened. We cannot defend or judge the people of the past; we were not living in their times. Charles Young, in Book One, gives a very apt description of relations between the Indian tribes, the United States Government, and the settlers in the West.

Given hundreds of books with stories like these, a reader could never come to a single conclusion about the Indians and the settlers. Individuals are just that: widely varied and unpredictable. All throughout history there were winners and losers, conquerors and conquered. America is about the youngest and the last in a long timeline of migrations.

As with each title I publish for Knowledge Keepers, spelling and grammar are original to the authors. The handful of footnotes in these books are also original.

I hope you enjoy these ordinary and priceless pieces of American history. If you haven't already, collect all the titles in the Knowledge Keepers Home Library series, and join me in preserving our history in print for generations to come.

Nicki Truesdell

Knowledge Keepers Bookstore, January 2022

BOOK ONE

DANGERS OF THE TRAIL
IN 1865

A Narrative of Actual Events

By CHARLES E. YOUNG

GENEVA, N. Y.

Press of W. F. Humphrey, Geneva, N. Y.
H. DeF. Patterson, Illustrator, Geneva, N. Y.

PREFACE

I present this narrative of actual events on a trip across the plains to Denver, Colorado, in 1865 and of life in the Far West in the later sixties.

An interesting and valuable feature is a map of the country, made in 1865, by Henry Bowles of Boston, showing the old Platte River and Smoky Hill Trails of that day before there was a railroad west of the Missouri River.

Everything is told in a plain but truthful manner, and this little volume is submitted to the reader for approval or criticism.

CHAS. E. YOUNG

July, 1912

CHAPTER I

"YOUNG MAN, GO WEST"

Early in 1859 gold was discovered in Colorado, and Horace Greeley, the well known writer and a power throughout the country both before and during the Civil War, made, in the interest of the *New York Tribune*, of which he was editor, an overland trip to Denver by the first stage line run in that day. He started from Leavenworth, Kansas, and with the exception of Mr. Richardson, of the *Boston Journal*, was the only passenger in the coach. The trip was not all that could be desired, for they met with numerous hardships and many narrow escapes, as did hundreds of others who had preceded them over that dangerous trail, many never reaching their destination—having met death at the hands of the cruel Indians of the plains.

During his stay in Denver Mr. Greeley wrote a number of letters to the *New York Tribune*, confirming the finding of gold in the territory and advising immigration. The people in the East were skeptical in regard to its discovery and awaited a written statement from him to this effect.

At the close of the war Mr. Greeley's advice to young men, through the columns of his paper, was to go West and grow up with the country, and it became a byword throughout the State of New York and the

Nation, "Young man, go West and grow up with the country."

Could Mr. Greeley have foreseen the number of young lives that were to be sacrificed through his advice, I think he would have hesitated before giving it; yet, it was the most valued utterance of any public man of that day for the settlement of the then Far West.

After reading a number of these letters in the *New York Tribune*, I became very enthusiastic over the opportunities that the West offered for the young man. There was also a loyal friend of mine who became as enthusiastic over it as myself. Thus, while we were still so young as to be called boys, we made up our minds to follow Mr. Greeley's advice, and "Go West and grow up with the country."

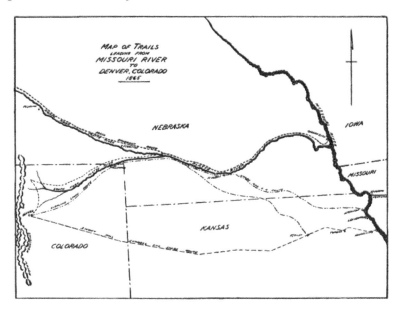

In making our purchases for the trip we were obliged to make our plans known to an acquaintance, who at once expressed a desire to accompany us. After consultation, we consented and at the appointed time, the fore part of July, 1865, just at the close of the Civil War, we boarded a New York Central train at the depot in Geneva, N. Y., with no thought of the hardships and dangers we would be called upon to meet.

The first night found us at the Falls of Niagara—the most stupendous production of nature that the country was known to possess at that time. Our time was divided between the American and Canadian sides, viewing the grand spectacle at all hours, from the rising to the setting of the sun; and, awed by the marvelous masterpiece of grandeur, we were held as if fascinated by its beauty, until we were forced to leave for the want of food and to replenish our commissary. When we boarded the cars to be whirled through the then wilds of Lower Canada, we were liberally supplied with the best the country produced.

Upon the fifth day we rolled into Chicago, the cosmopolitan city of the West. Two days later we reached Quincy, Ill., where we made connection with the old Hannibal & St. Joe Railroad which was to take us through Missouri to Atchison, Kansas. Missouri, after the war, was not an ideal state for a law abiding citizen, much less for inexperienced youths of our age, and we quickly realized that fact. Many stations had their quota of what was termed the Missouri bushwhacker, or, more plainly speaking, outlaws, who, during the war and for some time after, pillaged the state and surrounding country, leaving in their wake death and destruction. They had belonged to neither side at war, but were a set of villains banded together to plunder, burn, ravage and murder young and old alike;

as wicked a set of villains as the world has ever known. At many stations they would nearly fill the car, making it very unpleasant for the passengers. Their language and insults caused every one to be guarded in conversation. The condition of the road, however, often gave us relief, as we were obliged to alight and walk, at times, when arriving at a point where ties or rails had to be replaced. Its entire length showed the carnage and destruction of war, making travel slow and dangerous as well as uncomfortable. On reaching the state of bleeding Kansas and the then village of Atchison we were about used up. We at once called at the Ben Holiday Stage Office and inquired the price of a ticket to Denver, but finding it to be beyond our means, we decided to go by ox conveyance.

COMMANCHE BILL

We were not long in finding what, in those days, was called a tavern, located in the outskirts of the town. Having been chosen spokesman, I stepped up to the rough board counter and registered. We were soon confronted by the toughest individual we had yet seen. I pleasantly bade him good morning but received no immediate recognition, save a wild stare from two horrible, bloodshot eyes. I quickly came to the conclusion that we were up against the real Western article, nor was I mistaken. He didn't keep up waiting long, for he soon roared out an oath and wanted to know where we were from. After telling him as near as I possibly could, under the circumstances, he again became silent. His look and brace of revolvers were not reassuring, to say the least. He soon came out of his trance and did not keep us long in suspense, for his next act was to pull out both of his life-takers, and, not in very choice language, introduce himself as Commanche Bill from Arkansas, emphasizing the Arkansas by letting the contents of both of his instruments of death pierce the ceiling of his story and a half shack. I have wondered many times since that I am alive. We had been told by a fellow passenger that Atchison was a little short of Hades, and we were fast realizing that our informer was not far out of the way; yet, it was a haven in comparison to other places at which we were yet to arrive. Commanche William, or whatever his right name might have been, was a different person after his forceful introduction.

He began to question me. He asked me if we had any money.

"Yes."

"Any friends?"

"Certainly."

"Well, then you had better get straight back to them, for if you remain in these parts long, they will be unable to recognize you. Where are you fellows headed for, anyway?"

"Denver, Colorado."

"By stage?"

"No, sir. By ox or mule conveyance."

"You are too light weight. No freighter will hire you."

"They will or we'll walk."

"You will not walk far for the Indians along the Platte are ugly. By the way, do you pards ever take anything?"

Not wishing to offend such a character, I gave my companions the wink and we followed him into the bar-room with the full determination of making a friend of him. After all had done the sociable act—of course gentlemen only drink for sociability sake—I took him to one side purposely to draw him into a little private chat, and it was not long before his self-conceit had the better of him. He ordered grub—as all meals were called in the West in those days—for four, stating he was in need of a bite himself. Before the meal had been finished, I became convinced that the old fellow had a tender spot in his makeup, like all tough outlaws, and, if one had tact enough to discover it, he might have great influence over him; otherwise, we would be obliged to sleep with both eyes open and each with his right hand on the butt of his revolver.

THE AMERICAN INDIAN

The following day was passed in taking in the town and Indian Reservation, which was but a short distance from the place. There we came, for the first time, face to face with the American Indian, the sole owner of this vast and fertile continent before the paleface landed to dispute his right of ownership. Foot by foot they had been driven from East, North and South, until at that time they were nearly all west of the great Missouri River, or River of Mud, as the Indians called it. At the suggestion of our landlord, we took with us an interpreter, a few trinkets, and something to moisten the old chief's lips. Upon our arrival we were duly presented to the chief, who invited us to sit on the ground upon fur robes made from the pelts of different animals, including the antelope and the buffalo, or American bison, the monarch of the plains, and each one of us in turn took a pull at the pipe of peace. We then made a tour of their lodges. When we returned, the chief called his squaws to whom we presented our gifts, which pleased them greatly. To the old chief I handed a bottle of Atchison's best. As he grasped it, a smile stole over his ugly face, and with a healthy grunt and a broad grin, he handed me back the empty bottle. Indians love liquor better than they do their squaws. In return he gave me a buffalo robe which later became of great service. After taking another pull at the pipe of peace, we thanked him and took our departure, having no desire to be present when Atchison's invigorator commenced to invigorate his Indian brain.

The impression made by that visit to a supposedly friendly tribe, who at that time had a peace treaty with the government, was not one of confidence. The noble red men, as they were called by the Eastern philanthropist, were as treacherous to the whites as an ocean squall to the navigator. No pen or picture has or can fully describe the cruelty of their nature.

It was dusk when we reached our tavern, and we found it filled with a lawless band of degenerates, as repulsive as any that ever invested Western plains or canyons of the Rockies. We were at once surrounded and by a display of their shooting irons, forced to join in their beastly carnival. It was not for long, however, for a sign from the landlord brought me to his side. He whispered, "When I let my guns loose you fellows pike for the loft." There were no stairs. No sooner had he pulled his life-takers than all the others followed his example. Bullets flew in every direction. Clouds of smoke filled the room, but we had ducked and scaled the ladder to the loft and safety. Sleep was out of the question until the early hours of the morning, for the night was made hideous by blasphemous language, howls of pain and the ring of revolvers. The first call for grub found us ready and much in need of a nerve quieter, which the old sinner laughingly supplied; but no word from him of the night's bloody work. Taking me to one side, he said, "Take no offence, but repeat nothing you hear or see in these parts, and strictly mind your own business and a fellow like you will get into no trouble." I thanked him and followed his advice to the letter during my entire Western life.

THE FIRST CAMP

After that night's experience, we decided to pay our bill and become acclimated to camp life. We had taken with us a tent, blankets and three toy pistols, the latter entirely useless in that country, which proved how ignorant we were of Western ways. We were not long in finding a suitable camping spot a mile from the town and the same distance from the many corrals of the great Western freighters and pilgrims, as the immigrants were called. For miles we could see those immense, white covered prairie schooners in corral formation. Hundreds of oxen and mules were quietly grazing under the watchful eyes of their herders in saddle. It was certainly a novel sight to the tenderfoot.

We soon had our tent up and leaving one of our number in charge the other two went to town for the necessary camp utensils and grub. Immediately on our return supper was prepared and the novelty enjoyed. After a three days' rest I started out to make the rounds of the corrals in search of a driver's berth. All freighters had a wagon boss and an assistant who rightfully had the reputation of being tyrants when on the trail, using tact and discretion when in camp. A revolver settled all disputes. On approaching them they treated me as well as their rough natures would permit; but I did not take kindly to any of them. They all told me that I was undersized, and too young to stand the dangers and hardships of a trip. I returned to camp much disappointed but not discouraged.

The following morning we proceeded to the large warehouses on the river front, where all Western freighters were to be found. In those days all emigrants and oxen and mule trains with freight going to the far Western Territories would start from either Council Bluffs, Iowa, Leavenworth, Kansas, Atchison or St. Joe, Missouri; Atchison being the nearest point, a large majority embarked from there. The freight was brought up the Missouri River in flat-bottom steam-boats, propelled by a large wheel at the stern, and unloaded on the bank of the river. The perishable goods were placed in the large warehouses but the unperishable were covered with tarpaulin and left where unloaded. They were then transferred to large white covered prairie schooners and shipped to their different points of destination in trains of from twenty-five to one hundred wagons. The rate for freighting depended on the condition of the Indians and ran from ten cents per pound up to enormous charges in some cases.

SECURING PASSAGE

After making application to several of the freighters and receiving the same reply as from the wagon bosses, we went a short distance down the river to the last of the warehouses. On our approach we discovered a genuine bullwhacker—as all ox drivers were called in that day—in conversation with a short, stout-built fellow with red hair and whiskers to match. The moment he became disengaged I inquired if he was a freighter. He said that he was and that he wanted more men. His name was Whitehead, just the opposite to the color of his hair, and as I stepped up to him I wondered what kind of a disposition the combination made— whitehead, redhead. I at once made application for a position for the three of us. In rather a disagreeable voice, he asked me if I could drive. I replied that I could.

"Can you handle a gun and revolver?"

"Certainly."

"How many trips have you made?"

"None."

"Then how the devil do you know you can drive?"

"For the simple reason I am more than anxious to learn, and so are my friends." Then I made a clean breast of the position we were in and urged him to give us a chance.

"Well," he said, "You seem to be a determined little cuss; are the rest of the same timber?"

14

I told him they were of the same wood but not of the same tree.

After thinking the matter over, he said, "I'll tell you what I will do. I will hire the big fellow for driver at one hundred and twenty-five dollars per month, and the little fellow for night herder at one hundred dollars a month, and yourself for cook for one mess of twenty-five men and for driver in case of sickness or death, at one hundred and twenty-five dollars a month."

We then gave him our names, and, in return, he gave us a note to Mr. Perry, his wagon boss. We at once started for his corral, two miles distant, where we found the gentleman. He asked where our traps were. We told him, and also assured him that we would report for duty the following morning.

When we reached our camp we were completely tired out, but passed the remainder of the day in celebrating our success, and feeling assured that if we escaped the scalping knife of the Indians, we would reach Denver in due time, and, when paid off have a nice sum in dollars.

The following morning we had an early breakfast, broke camp, and reported at the corral where each was presented with two revolvers and a repeating carbine. I was then taken over to the mess wagon which was liberally supplied with bacon (in the rough), flour, beans, cargum (or sour molasses), coffee, salt, pepper, baking-powder and dried apples; the latter we were allowed three times a week for dessert. There was also a skillet for baking bread, which resembled a covered spider without a handle.

When the assistant cook, with whom I was favored, had started the fire and sufficient coals had accumulated, he would rake them out and place the skillet on them. As soon as the dough was prepared, a chunk was cut off and put in the skillet, the lid placed and covered with coals; in fifteen minutes we would have as nice a looking loaf of bread as one could wish to see, browned to a tempting color. When eaten warm, it was very palatable, but when cold, only bullwhackers could digest it. An old-fashioned iron kettle in which to stew the beans and boil the dried apples, or vice versa, coffee pots, frying pans, tin plates, cups, iron knives and forks, spoons and a combination dish and bread-pan made up the remainder of the cooking and eating utensils.

EXPERIENCES AMONG THE BUSHWHACKERS

It seemed that my assistant was exempt from bringing water, which often had to be carried in kegs for two miles, so he fried the meat and washed the dishes. I soon caught on to the cooking, and doing my best to please everyone, soon became aware of the fact that I had many friends among the toughest individuals on earth, the professional bullwhackers, who, according to their own minds, were very important personages. Their good qualities were few, and consisted of being a sure shot, and expert at lariat and whip-throwing. They would bet a tenderfoot a small sum that they could at a distance of twelve feet, abstract a small piece from his trousers without disturbing the flesh. They could do this trick nine times out of ten. The whips consisted of a hickory stalk two feet long, a lash twelve feet in length with buck or antelope skin snapper nine inches in length. The stalk was held in the left hand, the lash coiled with the right hand and index finger of the left. It was then whirled several times around the head, letting it shoot straight out and bringing it back with a quick jerk. It would strike wherever aimed, raising a dead-head ox nearly off its hind quarters and cutting through the hide and into the flesh. When thrown into space, it would make a report nearly as loud as a revolver. A lariat is a fifty foot line with a running noose at one end and made from the hide of various animals. It is coiled up and carried on the pommel of the saddle. When used for capturing animals or large game, it is whirled several times around the head when the horse is on a dead run and fired at the head of the victim. A professional can place the loop nearly every time.

During the third day of corral life, the steers arrived, and the hard work, mixed with much fun, commenced. A corral is about the shape of an egg, closed by the wagons at one end, and left open to admit the cattle at the other, then closed by chains.

MEANS OF TRANSPORTATION

Our wheelers and leaders were docile, old freighters, the others were long-horned, wild Texas steers. All of the freighters had their oxen branded for identification, using the first letter of his last name for the purpose. The brand was made from iron and was about four inches in height, attached to a rod three feet in length. A rope was placed over the horns of the animal and his head was drawn tight to the hub of a heavy laden prairie schooner. A bullwhacker, tightly grasping the tail of the beast, would twist him to attention. The man

17

with the branding implement heated to a white heat would quickly jab the ox on the hind quarter, burning through hair and hide and into the flesh. Then, after applying a solution of salt and water, he was left to recover as best he could. The brand would remain in evidence more than a year unless the steer was captured by cattle thieves, who possessed a secret for growing the hair again in six months. When the branding was completed, each man was given twelve steers to break to yoke, and it was three long weeks before we were in shape to proceed on our long Western tramp. The cattle were driven in each morning at break of day, the same time as when on trail. Each man with a yoke on his left shoulder and a bow in his right hand would go groping about in almost total darkness to select his twelve steers. When they were all found he would yoke them and hitch them to the wagons; the wheelers to the tongue, the leaders in front and the balance to section chains. For days we were obliged to lariat the wildest of them and draw their heads to the hubs of the heavily laden wagons, before being able to adjust the yoke, many times receiving a gentle reminder from the hind hoof of one of the critters to be more careful. I went into the fray with the full determination of learning the profession of driver and at the tenth day I had broken in a team of extras.

ON THE SICK LIST

I was then taken sick and for two long weeks kept my bed of earth under the mess wagon, with no mother or doctor, and two thousand miles from home. You may be able to imagine my feelings, but I doubt it. At the end of the second week Mr. Perry came and told me they would make a start the next afternoon and, in his judgment, he thought it unwise to think of making the trip in my present condition. I knew my condition was serious, but I would rather have died on the road, among those outlaws, than to have been left in Atchison among entire strangers. They were all very kind and did what they could for me, but were powerless to check my fast failing strength. I had wasted to less than one hundred pounds in weight and was too weak to even lift an arm.

I pleaded with Mr. Perry for some time and finally overcame his objections. "Well," he said, "Charlie, I will fix a bed in my wagon and you can bunk with me." I objected, for I did not wish to discommode him in the least and told him a good bed could be fixed in the mess wagon. "As you will," he said, and had the boys get some straw which together with the Buffalo robe made a very comfortable bed when not on the move.

A THUNDER STORM

The next day they picked me up and put me in the second or reserve mess wagon. Shortly after that the start was made. We had covered less than two miles when all of a sudden I heard the rumbling of distant thunder. Very soon rain began to patter on the canvas covering of my wagon. Then Heaven's artillery broke loose and the water came down in torrents. Never in my young life had I witnessed such a storm. It seemed as if thunder, lightning and clouds had descended to earth and were mad with anger. The racket was deafening. Between the angered claps could be heard the cursing of those Missouri bushwhackers, who, in their oaths, defied the Almighty to do his worst and hurled unspeakable insults at the memory of the mothers who gave them birth. I knew they were trying hard to make corral; whether they could do it, rested entirely with the wagon boss.

The cattle were crazed with fright and the moment they were loose, would certainly stampede. The oxen were finally unyoked and such a snorting and bellowing, it would be impossible to describe. As the racket died away in their mad race, my thoughts turned to my chum, who I knew was with them, and would be trampled beyond recognition by their death-dealing hoofs, if he had not gained his proper position in the rear.

THE LOG CABIN

At that juncture the front flaps of my wagon were parted and at a flash I recognized two of the men, who bore me across the way to the "Old Log Cabin" on the extreme edge of the then Western civilization. As they laid me down I swooned from sheer exhaustion and fright. Before I had become fully conscious I heard that gruff old wagon boss telling the good woman of the cabin to spare nothing for my comfort. She felt of my pulse, asked me a few questions and assured him that she would soon have me on my feet. He bade "God bless me," and passed out into the dark and stormy night. The good woman poked up the fire and placed an old-fashioned, iron tea-kettle in position to do its duty. At that juncture a young miss about my own age came from somewhere, as if by magic, and was told by the good mother to prepare a chicken, that she might make broth for the sick young man, pointing to where I lay. For two hours that good mother worked over me, now and then giving me draughts of hot herb tea, while the daughter deftly prepared nature's wild bird of the prairie, occasionally shooting darts of sympathy from her jet black eyes. When the bird had been cooked, the meat and bones were removed leaving only the broth which was seasoned to a nicety and given me in small quantities and at short intervals until early morning, when I passed into dreamland with the mother keeping vigil as though I were her own son. When I awoke I felt refreshed and comfortable, and found her still at my side, doing for me that which only a mother can.

At daybreak I heard footsteps above; presently the father and son came in. The daughter was called and breakfast was prepared. They told me that our cattle had stampeded and it might be days before they were found. After a three days search my chum and the cattle were overtaken miles from camp, but none the worse for their fearful experience. The moment he arrived he came to see me. I was sitting up for the first time, wrapped in Indian blankets, but very weak. I assured him that I would certainly get well, emphasizing the fact, however, that had we not run into that fearful storm, making my present haven of care possible, I could never have recovered, and believed that the prayers of a loving mother at home had been answered.

A CATTLE STAMPEDE

He then related his experience with those storm-maddened cattle. The first clap of thunder awoke him, and when the rain began he knew he was in for a bad night, and had taken every precaution to supply himself with all things needful. His description of the storm and mad race to keep up with those wild animals, crazed with fright, was enough to congeal the blood of a well man, and in my condition it nearly unnerved me. But I was delighted to know that he was safe, for we were like brothers. His safe arrival, together with the motherly care I had received and was receiving, put me rapidly on the gain. Not a morning passed that the daughter did not shoulder her trusty rifle and go out in search of some refreshment for me, always returning with a number of chickens of the prairie. She was a sure shot, as were the entire family, for they were all born and brought up on the border, moving farther West as the country became settled. From the father I learned the treachery of the Indians, their mode of warfare and different methods of attack; in fact, I had the devilish traits of the noble red men—as history called them—down to a nicety.

When the daughter's day's work was done, she would read to me and relate stories of her life, which reminded me of the "Wild Rose" in all its purity and strength.

The fifth day after the cattle were found the train broke corral and proceeded on its long Western tramp. Before leaving, Mr. Perry made arrangements with the old borderman for me to overtake them as soon as I was able.

The fourth day after the train had left, I made up my mind that I would start the next morning at sunrise and so informed my Western friends, whom, I felt, had saved my life. The old borderman expressed regret at my leaving and informed me that both he and his son would accompany me to camp. I thanked him and assured him that I felt a mother could not have done more for her own son than his wife had for me—they had all shown me every consideration possible—and that I should always remember them, which I have. At this juncture the mother spoke up gently, but firmly, and addressing her husband, said, "If you have no objection, daughter will accompany Mr. Young. She is a sure shot, a good horsewoman, and the horses are fleet of foot. We have not heard of any Indians in the neighborhood for some time, and besides she wants to go and the ride will do her good."

He replied, "My good woman, you cannot tell where the Indians are, they may be miles away today, but here this very night."

"That is true," she said, "but the stage driver told me that he had not seen a redskin since crossing the Nebraska line."

"That may be," he replied, "still they may have been in the bluffs, or sand hills watching their opportunity to surprise one of the many small trains of pilgrims, thinking to overpower them, run off their cattle and massacre all."

"Yes, that is all true, but I'll wager they could not catch our girl."

After thinking silently for a few moments, he said, "Well, if you wish, she may go; but if anything happens to our little one, you alone will be blamed."

That settled it. We talked long after father and brother had bade us good night. Mother and daughter finally retired; but, as for myself, I was nervous and restless, sleeping little, thinking of home and loved ones; not, however, forgetting the little "Wild Rose" that was separated from me only by a curtain partition.

The following morning we were up at break of day, and at just 5:30 on a lovely August morning the horses were brought to the door and both quickly mounted. Her riding habit of buckskin, trimmed with colored beads, was the most becoming costume I had ever seen on her during my stay, and for the first time I wished that I were not going, but it was for a moment only.

WITH THE WAGON TRAIN AGAIN

My destination was Denver, and nothing could change my plans except death in the natural way, or being cut down by those treacherous plains roamers. After a pleasant ride which lasted till noon, we came in sight of the corral. When within a quarter of a mile of it, she informed me she was going no farther. Both quickly dismounted. Our conversation would not interest you. Suffice to say, the parting was painful to both. I bade her good-bye and she was off like a flash. I walked slowly into camp, now and then turning to watch the fast retreating figure of as brave a prairie child as nature ever produced. The men appeared glad to see me; the gruff old wagon boss more so than any of the others, for he would not let me turn my hand to any kind of work until I was able. Then I did my best to repay him for his many kindnesses.

At 2 o'clock that afternoon the train broke corral, and for the first time I realized the slowness of our progress, and the long trip before us. Under the most favorable circumstances we could not make over ten miles a day and more often at the beginning three, five and seven.

Our bed was mother earth, a rubber blanket and buffalo robe the mattress, two pairs of blankets the covering, Heaven's canopy the roof; the stars our silent sentinels. The days were warm, the nights cool. We would go into camp at sundown. The cattle were unyoked and driven to water. After grub the night herder and one of the drivers would take them in charge, and if there were no Indians following, would drive them to a good grazing spot over the bluffs.

We passed through Kansas, after crossing the Little and Big Blue rivers, and part of Nebraska without seeing another log cabin or woods. Every fifteen or twenty miles there was a stage station of the Ben Holiday coach line, which ran between Atchison, Kansas, and Sacramento, California. At every station would be a relay of six horses, and by driving night and day would make one hundred miles every twenty-four hours. They were accompanied by a guard of United States soldiers on top of coaches and on horseback.

CHAPTER II

ARRIVAL AT FORT CARNEY

Arriving at Fort Carney we struck the Platte River trail leading to Denver. We were compelled by United States army officers to halt and await the arrival of a train of fifty armed men before being allowed to proceed. In a few hours the required number came up, together with three wagon loads of pilgrims. No train was permitted to pass a Government fort without one hundred well-armed men; but once beyond the fort, they would become separated and therein lay the danger.

A captain was appointed by the commander of the fort to take charge. Here we struck the plains proper, or the great American desert, as it was often called, the home of the desperate Indians, degraded half-breeds, and the squaw man—white men with Indian wives—who were at that time either French or Spanish; also the fearless hunters and trappers with nerves of steel, outdoing the bravest Indian in daring and the toughest grizzly in endurance. It is a matter of record that these men of iron were capable and some did amputate their own limbs. A knife sharpened as keen as a razor's edge would cut the flesh; another hacked into a saw would separate the bones and sensitive marrow; while an iron heated to white heat seared up the arteries and the trick was done. There was no anesthetic in those days.

There were also the cattle and mule thieves who lived in the bluffs, miles from the trail of white men, a tough lot of desperadoes, believing in the adage "Dead men tell no tales."

There were the ranchmen at intervals of twenty, fifty and a hundred miles, who sold to the pilgrims supplies, such as canned goods, playing cards, whiskey of the vilest type, and traded worn-out cattle, doctored to look well for a few days and then give out, thus cheating freighters and pilgrims alike.

These adobe ranches were built of sod cut in lengths of from two to four feet, four inches in thickness and eighteen inches in width and laid grass side down. The side walls were laid either single or double, six feet in height, with the end walls tapering upward. A long pole was then placed from peak to peak and shorter poles from side walls to ridge pole. Four inches of grass covered the poles and the same depth of earth completed the structure making the best fortifications ever devised; no bullet was able to penetrate their sides nor could fire burn them. The poles used for building these adobe ranches were in most cases hauled two hundred miles and in some cases three hundred miles.

WILD ANIMALS OF THE WEST

On a graceful slope roamed immense herds of buffalo, bands of elk, thousands of antelope, herds of black-and white-tail deer and the large gray wolf. Coyotes about the size of a shepherd dog would assemble on the high bluffs or invade the camp and make night hideous by their continuous and almost perfect imitation of a human baby's cry, making sleep impossible. The prairie dog, the fierce rattlesnake, and the beautiful little white burrowing-owl, occupied the same hole in the ground, making a queer family combination. Contrary to the belief of all dwellers and travelers of the plains in that day, Colonel Roosevelt claims it is not a fact that the three mentioned animals occupied the same quarters together, and that the story is a myth.

The little prairie dogs had their villages the same as the Indians. I have frequently seen a prairie dog come out and return into the same hole in the ground. I have also seen a beautiful little white owl silently perched at the side of the same hole and finally enter it, and a few moments later a fierce rattlesnake would crawl into the same hole. Whether it was the snake's permanent abode and it went in for a much needed rest, or whether it was an enemy to the others and the snake went in for a game supper of prairie dog puppies and owl squabs, departing by another route, I am unable to say, as I never took the trouble to investigate one of the holes to confirm the fact. If I had, I would in all probability still be digging. However, in this case, I am inclined to give Colonel Roosevelt the benefit of the doubt for the reason that if nature had not created an enemy to check their increase, the prairie dog would now over-run the country, as they multiply faster than any known animal, and are very destructive to the farm. The Government, through its agents, have destroyed thousands every year in the West by distributing poisoned grain. Last, but not least, of the life of the plains was the Pole Cat.

Conscious of his own ability to protect himself, he would often invade the camps at night, making the life of the sleeper miserable.

TROUBLE EN ROUTE

After leaving Fort Carney our troubles began. Many of the drivers were as treacherous as the Indians and would bear watching. One of them in our mess was a former bushwhacker, who bore many scars of his former unsavory life, one of which was the loss of an eye, which did not make him a very desirable acquaintance, much less a companion. He was of an ugly disposition, very seldom speaking to anyone and very few taking the trouble to speak to him. At times he acted as if he had been taking something stronger than coffee, but as we had not camped near any ranch where the poison could be procured, I came to the conclusion that he was a dope fiend. In some mysterious manner we had lost one of our cups, and at each meal for a week it fell to the lot of this particular bushwhacker to get left. He at last broke his long silence, and in anger with oaths, vowed he would not eat another meal without a cup, and would certainly take one from somebody, if obliged to. As soon as the call for grub was heard the next morning, all rushed simultaneously for a cup, and Mr. Bushwhacker got left again. Without ceremony he proceeded to make good his threat, the second cook being his victim.

For his trouble he received a stinging blow over his good eye, and was sent sprawling in the alkali dust. Not being in the least dismayed, he rushed for another and received a similar salute on the jaw, doubling him up and bringing him to the earth. By this time both messes joined in forming a ring and called for fair play. Mr. Perry tried hard to stop it, but was finally convinced that it was better policy to let them have it out. How many times the fellow was knocked down, I do not remember, but the last round finished him. We carried him to the shady side of his wagon, covered him with a blanket and resumed our meal. On going into corral, we always took our revolvers off and placed them where they could easily be reached. We had been eating but a short time, when the report of a gun rang out and each man fairly flew for his weapons. Indians seldom made an attack except at early morning, when the oxen were being yoked or when we were going into corral at night. To the surprise of everyone Mr. Bushwhacker had taken another lease of life and with a revolver in each hand was firing at anyone his disturbed brain suggested. He was quick of action, firing and reloading with rapidity, and soon had the entire camp playing hide and seek between, around and under the wagons to keep out of the range of his guns, which we succeeded in doing, for not a man was hit. Finally, two of the drivers succeeded in getting behind him and overpowered him. His brother bushwhackers were in for lynching him on the spot, but wiser council prevailed, and his disposal was left to Mr. Perry who sentenced him to be escorted back three miles from the corral and left to walk the remaining two miles to Fort Carney alone. He covered less than a mile when he was captured by the Indians. I was obliged then to drive his team. A few evenings later my chum and friend were lounging by the side of my wagon smoking, and otherwise passing the time away, when finally the conversation turned to the departed driver who by that time had undoubtedly been disposed of by the

Indians—not a very pleasant thought—but we consoled ourselves with the fact that no one was to blame but himself. My chum inquired the contents of my prairie schooner, and I replied that I did not know, but would investigate. Suiting the action to the word I crawled in, struck a match, and found a case labeled Hostetters' Bitters. Its ingredients were one drop of Bitters and the remainder, poor liquor. I soon found a case that had been opened, pulled out a bottle and sampled it. The old story came to me about the Irish saloonkeeper and his bartender. I called my chum and asked him if Murphy was good for a drink, he replied, "Has he got it?" "He has?" "He is then!" and we all were. I thought it would be impossible for the secret to be kept, but it was until we were on the last leg to Denver. The entire load consisted of cases of the Bitters. Fights were of frequent occurrence during the remainder of the trip, Mr. Perry being powerless to prevent them.

Arriving at Central City where the Bitters were consigned, the consignee reported to the freighter that the load just received consisted of one-half Bitters, the remainder Platte river water. Each man had twenty dollars deducted from his pay, and a large number of the drivers, in addition, bore earmarks of its effect.

The country from Fort Carney for four hundred miles up the Platte river valley and back from the high bluffs, that skirted the river on either side, was one vast rolling plain with no vegetation except a coarse luxuriant growth of grass in the valley near the river and beyond the bluffs; in spots that were not bare grew the prickly pear, and a short crisp grass of lightish color and of two varieties—the bunch and buffalo grasses—which were very nutritious, as the cattle thrived and

31

grew fat on them. There was the clear sky and sun by day, with an occasional sandstorm; the moon (when out) and stars by night, but no rain—a vast thirsty desert. On the small islands of the river a few scattered cottonwood trees were to be seen. Their high branches embraced a huge bunch of something that resembled the nest of an American Eagle, but on close inspection was found to be the corpse of a lone Indian a long time dead. This was the mode of burial of some of the tribes in the early days, using fur robes or blankets for a casket. There was nothing to relieve the monotony in this desert land, except desperate Indians, immense herds of animal life, daily coaches—when not held back or captured by the Indians or mountain highwaymen—returning freight trains, and the following points where there were adobe ranches: Dog Town, Plum Creek, Beaver Creek, Godfrey's, Moore's, Brever's at Old California Crossing and Jack Morrow's at the junction of the north and south Platte, Fort Julesburg, Cotton Wood and the Junction, each one hundred miles apart, and John Corlew's and William Kirby near O'Fallow's Bluffs. It was said of these ranchmen that some were honest and some were not; others were in league with the Indians, and cattle and mule thieves, and, as a rule, a bad lot. They traded supplies to the Indians for furs of every kind. The winter passed in hunting, trapping, drinking, and gambling.

O'FALLOW'S BLUFFS

O'Fallow's Bluffs was a point where the river ran to the very foot of the bluffs making it necessary for all of the trains to cross, then again strike Platte river trail at Alkali Creek, the waters of which were poisonous to man and beast. The trail over the bluffs was of sand, and those heavily ladened, white covered prairie schooners would often sink to the hubs, requiring from fifty to seventy-five yoke of oxen to haul them across, often being compelled to double the leading yoke as far back as the wheelers, then doubling again, would start them on a trot, and with all in line and pulling together, would land the deeply sunken wheels on solid ground. It took one entire day to again reach river trail, which was hard and smooth. O'Fallow's Bluffs was a point feared by freighters and emigrants alike. At this point many a band of pilgrims met destruction at the hands of the fiendish redskins of the plains. Directly upon going into camp at night a party of them would ride up, demand coffee, whiskey, or whatever they wanted, and having received it, would massacre the men and children, reserving the women for a fate a thousand fold worse, as they were very seldom rescued by the tardy government, whose agents were supplying the Indians with guns, ammunition and whiskey to carry on their hellish work unmolested. When captured, which was seldom, were they hung as they deserved? No, the chief with a few others, who stood high in the councils of the tribe, were taken by stage to Atchison, Kansas, there transferred to luxuriantly equipped sleeping cars of that day, and whirled on to Washington; and, in war paint and feather and with great pomp, were presented to their great white father (the President) as they called him.

ABUSES OF THE INDIAN DEPARTMENT

They were then taken in charge by Representatives of the Indian department of the Government, that in those days was honeycombed with corruption from foundation to dome; a disgraceful and blood-stained spot in the Nation's history. Day after day and night after night they were shown the sights of that great city. The capitol of a free and growing Republic whose people respected the Constitution their fathers had drafted, signed and fought for. Day after day and night after night they were courted, dined, toasted and wined until they had become sufficiently mellow to be cajoled into signing another peace treaty, and were then given money and loaded down with presents as an inducement to be good. They were then returned to the agency at the Fort, having been taken from there and back by those red-nosed, liquor-bloated Indian Department guardians of the United States Government and were freely supplied with whiskey until they were willing to part with their cattle, furs, and beaded goods at extremely low figures, in exchange for provisions, guns, ammunition, and liquor at fabulously high prices. Robbed of their money and presents, and in this condition allowed to return to their village, where when they become sober, they would quickly awaken to a realizing sense of how they had been deceived, swindled and robbed.

What could you expect from those copper-colored savages of the soil after such treatment? With no regard for the treaty they had signed, they would resume the warpath. Revenge, swift and terrible, was meted out to the innocent pilgrims and freighters who had left home, comforts and friends. Hundreds sacrificed their lives by horrible tortures in their heroic efforts to settle the West, unconscious that they were making history for their country and the nation, great.

With no respect for the United States Government, with no respect for the flag with its cluster of stars and stripes of red, white and blue that fired the heart of every living American soldier to win victory at Valley Forge, which gained our independence, Antietam, and San Juan Hill, saved the nation, reunited the union of states in lasting friendship, lifted the yoke of tyranny from an oppressed people; and, as if with one stroke, swept from the high seas two powerful naval squadrons—the pride of the Spanish nation.

Washington, Lincoln and McKinley were backed by the old glory that electrified every loyal American with patriotism to respond to the call of duty for the love of their country and the "Star Spangled Banner," that at that time fluttered high above the parapet of every Government fort as an emblem of protection to all that were struggling on and on over that vast expanse of unbroken and treeless plain; can you wonder then that the unspeakable crimes and mistakes of the Government of those days still rankle in the breast of every living man and woman that in any way participated in the settlement of the West? If you do, look on the painting of the terrible annihilation of the gallant Custer and his five companies of the Seventh U. S. Cavalry with the old chief, Sitting Bull, and his band of Sioux Indians on the Big Horn River, June 25, 1876, from which not a man escaped to tell the tale, and you may form some conception of the hardships, suffering, and cruelties inflicted on the early pioneer. It was left for the resourceful Remington to vividly portray life and scenes of those days, perpetuating their memory on canvas and bronze for all time. The name of Frederick Remington should not only go down in history as the greatest living artist of those scenes, but his bust in bronze should be given a place in the Hall of Fame as a tribute to his life and a recognition of his great worth.

CHAPTER III

AN ATTACK BY THE INDIANS

'Fallow's Bluffs was the most dismal spot on the entire trail. Its high walls of earth and over-hanging, jagged rocks, with openings to the rolling plain beyond, made it an ideal point for the sneaking, cowardly savages to attack the weary pilgrims and freighters. The very atmosphere seemed to produce a feeling of gloom and approaching disaster. The emigrants had been repeatedly instructed by the commander at Fort Carney to corral with one of the trains. Many of the bullwhackers were desperate men, so that the poor pilgrims were in danger from two sources, and very seldom camped near either corral. Our consort was a day's drive in the rear. That evening the emigrants camped about a half mile in advance of our train. It was at this point, when unyoking our oxen at evening that a large band sneaked over the bluffs for the purpose, as we supposed, of stampeding our cattle. They did not take us unawares, however, for we never turned cattle from corral until the assistant wagon boss surveyed the locality in every direction with a field glass, for the tricky redskin might be over the next sand hill.

Fifty good men could whip five times their number, especially when fortified by those immense white covered prairie schooners in corral formation. On they came in single file, their blood-curdling war whoop enough to weaken the bravest. Closer they came, bedecked in war-paint and feathers, their chief in the lead resembling the devil incarnate with all his aids bent on exterminating as brave a band of freighters as ever crossed the plains. Nearer they came, their ponies on a dead run, the left leg over the back, the right under and interlocking the left, firing from the opposite side of them, ducking their heads, encircling the camp and yelling like demons. Their racket, together with the yelping of their mongrel dogs and the snorting and bellowing of the cattle, made it an unspeakable hell. Every man stood to his gun, and from between the wagons, at the command of the wagon boss, poured forth with lightning rapidity his leaden messengers of death. For about an hour they made it very interesting for us. It was almost impossible to hit one as they kept circling the camp, drawing nearer with each circle made. How many were killed we did not know as they carried them off, but from the number of riderless ponies, a dozen or more must have been dispatched to their happy hunting grounds. During the fight a portion of them bore down on the poor pilgrims' camp, in plain sight, and massacred all, running off their cattle and such of their outfit as they wanted.

SAVAGES IN THEIR GLORY

Mothers with babes at their sides and with uplifted, clasped hands, implored the cruel warriors for mercy, but it was like pouring water on the desert sands. Crazed by thirst for blood and the scalps of the whites, they knew no mercy. The hatchet-like tomahawk glittering in the evening twilight, held with a vice-like grip in the hand of a cowardly savage, came down at last with such force as to crush through skull and brain, and all was over. We were powerless to render assistance. The scene was heartrending. The depredations of these savages is too revolting to relate, and after completing their hellish work, they sneaked back as they came, keeping up their sickening yell until distance drowned it entirely. Few days passed that they were not seen as evening approached, and after dark we were able to know that they were in the vicinity, watching their opportunity to surprise us at early morning, by signal arrows of fire shot into the heavens to make known their whereabouts to companions. Could these silent bluffs of sand but unfold the butchery and unspeakable outrages inflicted on innocent men, women and children, could the trail through the valley of the Platte, and even more dangerous trail of the Smoky Hill give up its secrets, it would reveal a dark page in the history of our Government, which was directly responsible for a great deal of it; responsible in so far as sending unscrupulous peace commissioners to the different agencies to make treaties of peace with tribes of Indians, and who kept them just long enough to become liberally supplied with provisions, clothing, guns, ammunition and whiskey, then ravish and murder in the most diabolical manner pilgrims and freighters alike. On both trails many a silent monument of stone was all that remained of their cruel depredations. Such was not the uncommon work of the fiends, known to readers of fiction as the noble red men of the plains. More dastardly cowards never existed. Their struggles against destiny have long since been broken, and the offspring of those cruel warriors are being educated by a gracious government.

The monotony of that lonesome and tedious tramp was enlivened only by fights among the men, and an occasional lay-over for a day to set the tires of the many wagons, having had no rain to keep them tight during the entire trip after leaving Atchison, Kansas.

With many encounters and bearing scars received from warring tribes of Indians, we tramped along in moccasin covered feet, now and again throwing our long lashed whips with such force as to awaken the dead-head ox to life and quicker action.

Day after day the same scenery faced us; yet, it was an experience never to be forgotten. We passed Fort Julesburg and Cottonwood with the loss of but three men, arriving late at night after a forced drive at the junction or division of the two trails leading to Denver. The distance to Denver by the "Cut-off" was seventy-five miles; by the river route one hundred miles; but as water was to be found only at long distances on the former, all cattle trains took the river route.

It was early in November, the nights and mornings were cold and frosty, the air exhilarating. We were up the next morning at the usual time, and as the sun rose in all its splendor and warmth, one hundred miles in the far away distance could be seen with the naked eye, the gigantic range of the Rockies whose lofty snow-capped peaks, sparkling in the morning sun, seemed to soar and pierce the clouds of delicate shades that floated in space about them, attracted, as it were, by a heavenly magnet. It was a sight I had not dreamed of, and one that made an impression on my young mind to last through life.

DENVER AT LAST!

When about ten miles from Denver—so we at least thought, and fearless of danger, my chum and myself obtained permission from Mr. Perry to walk to the city over the rolling ground. We tramped until the sun was well up in the heavens. One would think it but a few miles to those mighty and solemn mountains of rocks, so deceptive was the distance, yet, they were twenty miles beyond the city. At noon we knew we had made ten long miles and were completely tired out. We were on the point of taking a rest when I urged my chum to cross the next knoll, and if the city did not loom up we would halt. We did so and to our surprise and joy were right in the city of Denver, the "Mecca" of nearly all Western freighters and distributing point for the far Western territories. It seemed to have risen beneath our feet. The grand old range of mountains with their sky-soaring pinnacles and scenic background of grandeur, together with the surrounding landscape, made it the sight of one's life. Our sixteen mile walk and previous seventy days' living on a diet of bacon, beans, and dried apples, certainly placed us in condition for a civilized meal.

We were directed to a first-class restaurant, both in price and quality of food. We were about famished, and to satisfy our hunger seemed impossible. We ate and ate, and probably would have been eating yet, had not the waiter presented us with a ticket demanding a five dollar gold piece from each, when we decided we had better call a halt, if we intended to remain in the city over night.

AN OLD ACQUAINTANCE

On walking up the street we stepped into the first hotel we came to, the old "Planters," registered, paid for our supper, lodging and breakfast. When about to

leave the hotel, who should walk in but a Genevan by name, Michael C. Pembroke, with his arm in a sling. He had been propelled across the plains by mules, and one of the ugly brutes had broken his right arm with one of his ever active hoofs. I asked Michael why the mule kicked him? He replied, "Charlie, I may look foolish but was not fool enough to go back and ask him." Never approach a Missouri

Michael C. Pembroke

mule from the rear, for there certainly will be trouble if you do. He asked if we had any money.

We replied that we would have when paid off.

He advised us to go direct to the Ben Holiday stage office and buy a ticket for the States as soon as we received our pay, as Colorado was no place for boys.

At his suggestion we started out to do the town, and came very near being done ourselves. Colorado at this time was a territory with a Governor appointed by the

President. Law, except as executed by a vigilance committee, did not amount to much more than the word. If one wished to depart life in full dress, he could be accommodated by simply calling another a liar or cheat at gambling. If desirous of taking a long rest by being suspended by the neck from a limb of the only tree in Denver at that time, which was on the west side of Cherry Creek, all he had to do was to appropriate to himself an ox, mule, or anything of value, and the vigilance committee would manipulate the rope.

The gambling places, which occupied long halls on the ground floor of tall buildings—nearly always on the business street of the city—kept open until the small hours of morning. There was always a brass band in front, and a string band, or orchestra, in the extreme rear, so if one wished to dance, he could select a partner of most any nationality; dance a set, step up to the bar, pay two bits or twenty-five cents for cigars, drinks or both and expend his balance on any game known to the profession, which games occupied either side of the long room.

We had been in the place less than fifteen minutes when bang went a revolver and on the instant the room was in total darkness. I mechanically ducked under a table. Where my companions were, I knew not; I began to think that Mike's advice was about correct, and before emerging wished more than once I was back in my home. When the lights were turned on, I discovered my chum occupying a like berth of safety on the opposite side of the room.

Mike had evidently followed his own advice and taken his departure, for he was nowhere to be found.

The band struck up a lively tune; the fiddles, a waltz; dancing began, gold and chips commenced to fly, and, if I had not passed through the ordeal, I never would have known anything had happened. The dead were quickly disposed of, the wounded hurried to physicians, and old timers gave it no further thought, as it was of frequent occurrence, and one soon became hardened. Denver at that time was a hotbed of gambling, with murder and lynch law a secondary pastime. Not being deterred by our experience, we continued our sightseeing, ending up at the only theatre in the city, afterwards called the "Old Languish."

JOINING THE CATTLE TRAIN AGAIN

The following afternoon our train reached town and we joined it during the evening to be ready for an early start for Golden City, the entrance to the mountains leading to Black Hawk and Central City where our freight was consigned. The most hazardous part of our trip was before us, one that to this day makes me shiver when I think of it. The first team entered the canyon at 11 A. M. in a blinding snowstorm. The road for nearly the entire distance was hewn from solid rock out of the side of steep mountains, gradually ascending to a great height, then descending to what seemed a bottomless canyon. We finally arrived at Guy Hill, the most dangerous part of the route. It took us one entire day to reach its pinnacle, where we camped for the night. The road at the top was cut through solid rock at a height of twenty feet, seven feet in width and led to a steep precipice. It then made a sharp turn to the right and, in a serpent shape drive, continued to the canyon below. At this point it was said to be fifteen hundred feet

44

straight down, and a number of outfits had previously gone over its rocky edge and been hurled to destruction by a slight error of judgment on the part of the driver.

The cold and snow, together with summer clothing, made our suffering indescribable. The following morning I started in the lead of the train with a nine thousand pound boiler, with the rear wheels securely locked, and twenty yoke of oxen to haul it to the edge of the precipice. Then discarding all but the wheelers and leaders, we began the descent. There was not room enough on either side for the driver to walk. He generally rode the off ox, but I took my position on the rear of the wagon tongue and found it decidedly the safest place in case of an accident. By night all wagons were safely in the canyon below. The road for nearly the entire distance presented the same dangers, taking ten days to reach our destination from Denver, the entire trip occupying eighty days.

A THRILLING COACH RIDE

On receiving our pay, which was our promised salary less twenty dollars for the Hostetter's Bitters, my chum and myself decided to go direct to Denver, our friend remaining in the Mountain City. We boarded a Concord coach with six snow-white horses to wheel us on a dead run over and around steep mountains and through dismal canyons, first on four wheels, then three, then two and occasionally one, keeping us constantly busy retaining our seats and fearing at every turn that we would be dashed into eternity; and yet, it was one of the most picturesque and thrilling rides one could take. Being tossed from side to side in the roomy coach, now and then grabbing a fellow passenger with desperation, gazing down from lofty peaks to yawning chasms below, hearing the crack of the long-lashed whip urging the noble steeds to faster speed, turning the rough, ragged, serpent-shaped drive, thundering through clouds and mist with lightning rapidity, and always in constant terror of a breakdown or error on the part of the fearless driver, gave one a sensation that would nearly make his hair stand on end. During the descent a slight error on the part of the horses or driver, would have hurled all to a horrible death; but those mountain drivers, strapped to their seats, were monarchs of the Rockies and unerring in every move. From among the snow-covered glaciers sparkling in the morning sun, emitting the many tints of a midday storm-bow and presenting a sight of unsurpassed grandeur, we emerged from the mouth of the last canyon and struck the smooth rolling trail. All the way from Golden we were going, it seemed, on the wings of the wind and were landed in Denver on scheduled time.

CHAPTER IV

DENVER IN 1865

In that period Denver was appropriately called the "City of the Plains." Situated sixteen miles from the base of the nearest Rocky Mountain peak, and six hundred and fifty miles from Atchison, Kansas, the nearest town to the East; while seven hundred miles to the west loomed up as from the very bowels of the earth, the beautiful city of the Mormons, Salt Lake City, Utah. The nearest forts—two hundred miles distant—were Fort Cottonwood to the northeast, Collins to the north and Halleck to the northwest. Its northern limits extended to the South fork of the Platte River; Cherry Creek running through one-third, dividing it into East and West Denver. Its population numbered about five thousand souls. Here was to be found the illiterate man—but a grade above the coyote—lawbreakers of every kind and from every land, to men of culture and refinement. Here it stood, a typical mining town, a monument to the indomitable energy of man in his efforts to settle that barren and almost endless plain and open to the world the Rocky's unlimited hidden gold. Here were brick structures modern for that day, the brick being made from the soil of the territory; a United States mint, a church, a school house, large warehouses, stores, and the home of the *Rocky Mountain Daily News*, which kept one partially in touch with happenings in the faraway states. Isolated from the outside world, it was an ideal place of refuge for those anxious to escape the outraged law. Knights of the green cloth held full sway. Men in every walk in life gambled. A dead man for breakfast was not an uncommon heading for the menu card, the old tree on the west bank of Cherry Creek furnishing the man. Society was just a little exclusive and to gain admission the pass was, "Where are you from?" and in some cases, "Your name in the East."

Desperadoes made one attempt to lay the city in ashes and certainly would have accomplished their purpose had it not been for the timely action of the Vigilance Committee in hanging the ring-leaders. When the guilt of a suspect for any crime was in doubt, he was presented with a horse or mule and ordered to leave between sun and sun and never return. During my four years of residence in Denver there was but one Indian scare and it made a lasting impression on the tablet of my memory. A church bell pealed forth the warning over the thirsty desert of an Indian attack. Business places were closed, the women and children were rushed to the mint and warehouses for protection, armed men surrounded the city, pickets on horseback were thrown out in every direction. Couriers kept thundering back and forth between picket line and those in command and others were despatched to the different Forts for assistance that never came. A look of determination stood out on the face of every one and not a man, from clergyman to desperado, within the confines of the city who would not willingly have given up his life's blood to protect the honor of the women and lives of the little ones. For three weary days and the same number of nights the terrible suspense lasted, but no Indian came. It was a false alarm.

Denver, in its early settlement, was never attacked by the Indians except in isolated cases. The only reason that I ever heard given for their not doing so was that they knew not their strength, for there was no time in the sixties that they could not have swooped down on the place, massacred all and buried the little mining town in ashes.

SECURED WORK AGAIN

For a young man to obtain work other than oxen or mule driving, we were told, was simply impossible. Not being deterred, however, by this discouraging information we at once started out to secure work. Board was twenty-five dollars a week in gold, and you had to furnish your own sleeping quarters, so not to secure work at once would quickly reduce our wealth. We had called on nearly all of the business places, when my chum secured a position with a grocer and freighter. As for myself, I received little encouragement but finally called at a large restaurant where I was offered work. I told the proprietor it was a little out of my line, but he told me that if I could not find a position to suit me, I should walk in at any time, pull off my coat and go to work, which I did three days later. About the tenth day the proprietor told me his lease expired and that the man who owned the building was going to conduct the business. He came in that afternoon, and I was introduced to him. Before leaving he stepped into the office and informed me that he wanted a man next to him; or, in other words, an assistant and that the former proprietor had given me a good recommend and he thought that I would suit him. He made me a tempting offer and I accepted. The restaurant was located on Blake street, one of the then principal business streets of the city, and kept open until early morning as did the gambling places in the immediate vicinity. I soon discovered that the new proprietor could neither read or write and that he conducted one of the largest private club rooms in the city where gambling was carried on without limit. He paid me a large salary and allowed me everything my wild nature craved. I had charge of the entire business as well as his bank account.

The restaurant was the headquarters of nearly all oxen and mule drivers and also of the miners who came from the mountains in winter, and were of the toughest type of men of that day. All professional oxen and mule drivers after making one round trip to the river and points in the far Western territories were paid off in Denver and many of them would deposit with me, for safe keeping, a large share of their dangerously and hard earned dollars. They would then start out to do the town, now and then taking a chance at one of the many gambling games, always returning for more money, which I would give them; and this they would continue until all was expended except enough to keep them a week, when sober, and a commission for doing the business, for which I was careful to look out. An individual who bore the name of "One Eye Jack" boarded with us and I could always depend upon him in time of trouble. His vocation for a long time was a mystery, until one evening, as I was passing down a side street, he popped out from an alley and with

50

uplifted blackjack would have felled and robbed me had he not recognized the unearthly yell I gave. I forgave him, and afterwards he doubled his energies to protect me and on more than one occasion saved my life. When in his professional clothes he was a tough looking customer and could fight like a bull dog. He was always liberally supplied with someone else's money. Yet with all his bad traits, his word was as good as his gold; but like other similar individuals that infested Denver at that time, he finally went to the end of his tether, and was presented by the Vigilance Committee with a hemp collar that deprived him of his life.

Before his demise, however, a party of ten tough-looking individuals entered the restaurant and, in forceful language, demanded the best the country offered in eatables and drink. My friend, or would-be-murderer, was in at the time and I noticed a look of cunning pleasure steal over his rough countenance. The strangers were dressed in corduroy trousers, velveteen coats, slouch hats and black ties. Their shirts and collars of red flannel made a conspicuous appearance and caused their undoing later. After seeing them well cared for, I returned to the office and calling Jack inquired his opinion of the gents.

"Well," he replied, "I may be mistaken but I will just bet you a ten spot they are road agents." "Yes," I said, "I am inclined to agree with you, but keep mum."

You may think it strange I did not give this bold highwayman away; but life in those days was sweet and I had no desire to have that young life taken so I followed Commanche Bill's advice and strictly

51

minded my own business. If I had not, I would not be living today.

HIGHWAYMEN OF THE WEST

Two mornings later on entering for breakfast one of the band had his head done up in a bandage. From words he dropped I was satisfied that Jack or one of his cronies had been improving their spare time by relieving him of his over abundance of gold. The reckless manner in which they disposed of their money and their conversation when flushed with wine betrayed their true characters and stamped them a murderous band of mountain highwaymen who had made their headquarters in the fastnesses of the Rockies, near the overland mountain trail and there devoted their time to holding up stage coaches, compelling the driver with a shot from a carbine to halt, descend, disarm and be quiet. The passengers were then ordered to alight and stand in a row, continually being covered with guns by a part of the band and by others relieved of their personal effects. Then the stage coach was systematically gone through together with the Wells Fargo & Co's. safe, which often contained gold into the thousands. These hold-ups were not infrequent and were the fear of all who were obliged to pass through these canyons of robbery and often death. The bunch that we harbored were undoubtedly as bold a band of robbers and murderers as ever infested the silent caves of the Rockies. Could their dingy walls but talk they would reveal crimes unspeakable. I knew there were many strangers in town and was almost certain their every movement was watched; nor was I mistaken. The seventh day after their arrival a young school teacher whom I knew by sight called at the restaurant and inquired by name for one of the band. I asked if he knew him. He replied, no more than that he had met him in one of the corrals of the city and had been offered free passage to the States if he would do their cooking. I told him of my suspicions and all I knew about them and advised him not to go with them, but like many others he gave no heed. Two days later they were missed at meal time. The next morning word came by courier that the entire band including the school teacher were dangling by the neck from the branches of cottonwood trees twelve miles down the Platte River with their pockets inside-out and outfits gone. Thus was meted out innocent and guilty alike the Vigilance Committee justice, which was not of uncommon occurrence.

Mr. Pembroke secured a position at Black Hawk, Colorado, in the year 1865, with the first smelter works erected in the Rocky Mountains. He was employed in the separating department where sulphur was freely used, and he inhaled much of the fumes emitted therefrom, which was the direct cause of a severe illness.

He fought retirement for a long time, but was finally forced to give up.

The latter part of February, 1886, he arrived in Denver on his way to his home in Geneva, N. Y., but remained with me at the restaurant for ten days where he was cared for and given the best of medical aid available in those days.

He finally prevailed on a mule freighter to take him as a passenger to Atchison, Kansas. Arriving at Fort

Carney, Nebraska, he had a relapse and was ordered by the Commander of the Fort to be placed in the Army Hospital for treatment, where he remained until able to continue his journey by stage to Atchison, thence by rail home.

He left Colorado with the full determination of returning on recovering his health. A mother's influence, however, changed his plans and he finally decided to remain in the East. He purchased a grocery business and conducted it with great success until his death, March 17th, 1910. By his strict attention to business, square dealing, genial disposition and original wit, he gained the confidence and respect of his fellow-men. He was buried in St. Patrick's cemetery in his home city where a surviving sister has caused to be erected an appropriate and costly monument to his memory.

NEW EMPLOYMENT

I remained with the restaurant keeper one year, when through the assistance of influential men that boarded at the restaurant, I secured a position with a grocer. Shortly after entering his employ I made the acquaintance of an ex-army officer, a graduate of West Point and a well educated man, who afterwards became my boon companion. At that time he was an ex-pork merchant from Cincinnati; an eccentric old fellow without chick or child, and with plenty of money to loan at 3% a month. He owned a large warehouse on Cherry Creek in West Denver where he slept and did his own cooking. His evenings were passed at the store and many were the nights that we told stories and otherwise enjoyed ourselves. He was a silent member of the firm and I was wise enough to keep on the right side of him. During that time the head of the firm ran for Congress on the Democratic ticket. Such an election I never want to see or go through again. Large wagons loaded with barrels of all kinds of liquor on tap were driven from poll to poll. Many more ballots were cast in each precinct than there were voters and by night nearly the entire male portion of the inhabitants were a drunken, howling mass. The outcome of the election resulted in the Governor giving the Democratic nominee the certificate of election; the Secretary of the territory favoring the Republicans. The Governor left the city that night and never returned. The contest terminated in a Republican Congress seating the Republican candidate, and Andrew Johnson—then President of the United States—appointing the Democratic candidate Governor of Colorado. A year from that time General Grant was inaugurated, and shortly afterwards the Governor's head went into the basket and mine fell on the outside.

On another occasion there was to be a prize fight at Golden City, sixteen miles from Denver. My friend, the ex-pork merchant, I could see was anxious to attend but did not wish to lower his standard of dignity by doing so, so the subject was not mentioned save in a casual way until the morning of the fight, when he entered the store, puffing and blowing, stamping the floor with his hickory cane and mopping his crimson brow with an old-fashioned bandana handkerchief, said "Charley, let's go to that infernal fight. I don't approve of it, but let's go."

"All right," I said. I was in for any kind of sport.

AN EXPERIENCE IN MULE RIDING

I left everything, locked the store and started out to procure a rig, but found there were none to be had for love or money. The only article of propulsion we could hire were saddle mules. Both quickly mounted and on a slow trot started for the ring. We had been there less than an hour when both of us became thoroughly disgusted and started on the return trip. When about seven miles from Denver and going at a lively pace— for a mule—the Major's animal stiffened both front legs, and placing his hoofs firmly in the sandy road, permitted the Major's chunky little body to pass over his head and through space for about ten feet, landing, with much force, on his stomach. The old fellow was an artist at curse words and the more I laughed the more he cursed. He was a sprightly little fellow and on gaining his feet grabbed for the bridle, but Mr. Mule shook his head, made a side step, and the devil could not have caught him again until he reached the barn. I dismounted and with much difficulty my friend scrambled into my saddle, with myself on behind. But my long-eared critter objected and the fun commenced. He bunted and kicked. All of a sudden his hind quarters rose and like lightning his long lanky legs shot high into the air. First, I went off, and on gaining a sitting position with mouth, ears and eyes full of sand, I witnessed a spectacle befitting the clumsiest bareback rider on one of their first lessons. The old Major had both arms affectionately entwined around the mule's thick neck and was hanging on with desperation. Up and down went the hind quarters of that unkind brute, bunting and kicking, the Major's little body keeping taps with the ups and downs and every time he caught his breath he let out a war whoop that would do credit to a Commanche brave. The old mule finally dumped him all in a heap and followed his mate to Denver. Such an appearance as both presented, each blaming the other for our misfortune and vowing we would never be caught at another prize fight. Lame, bruised, and crestfallen, we walked the remainder of the way into Denver. Each cautioned the other to say nothing of our misfortune; but the two Mauds had carried the news ahead, and we were the laughing stock of the town for the next nine days.

At another time I was attending a performance in the "Old Languish Theater," when from the stage I was informed I was wanted in the bar room of the building, a necessary adjunct to all western theaters in those days. Upon entering I was taken by the hand by one of those trusty and warm-hearted stage drivers of the plains and Rockies, and told that my chum had been caught in one of those treacherous mountain snow storms on the Catchla Purder River two miles above La Port and was badly frozen, and, if he didn't receive medical aid at once, could not survive. I left the theater at once and commenced preparing plans for the trip. I started unaccompanied the following afternoon at 2:30 o'clock on a one hundred fifty mile ride.

A RIDE IN A STORM

My conveyance was a long old-fashioned buggy. The buggy, which was well filled with straw, blankets, medicine, grub, and a commissary bottle, had two good roadsters hitched in front to wheel me to the rescue of my friend or to an ignominious death. I had not only Indians to fear, but the treacherous elements. The trail ran close along the base of the mountains. It was a lovely May day. I was obliged to make thirty-two miles that night to reach cover. Less than half of the distance had been traveled when the wind veered suddenly to the north, mild at first, then a hurricane of anger, roaring and blowing with such force as to nearly upset the buggy. Dark clouds gathered and floated around those silent peaks of ages. Lightning darted hither and thither among the stalwart pines, which were creaking, bending and crashing. Clap after clap of thunder pealed through and from those dismal canyons, vibrating between Nature's slopes of granite, quartz and rock. The din was fearful, rain fell at first, then turned to snow. Just before it became dark I adjusted the front piece of the buggy. My compass was useless. I urged my faithful steeds to faster speed, and at the same time gave them the rein. As I did so, they left the trail. Cold and chilled to the marrow or very bone, I took frequent drafts from the commissary bottle, and fought with all my power against sleep, but it was useless.

On gaining partial consciousness two squaws were bending over me rubbing me with all their Indian strength and a third forcing something warm down my throat. Men, rough of dress, were smoking and playing cards. Revolvers, chips and gold was in front of each, with plenty of the latter in the center of the table. I knew not if they were friends or mountain highwaymen. Many claim that horses are dumb brutes with no instinct, but that faithful pair on leaving the trail avoided a long bend and made straight for the adobe stage ranch, sixteen miles away. On reaching it, they ran the buggy-pole through the only opening of that mud shack rousing the inmates to action and bringing me to safety.

The large Concord coach filled with passengers soon arrived from Denver, and owing to the severity of the storm, put up for the night. The time was passed in smoking, drinking and playing cards. At six o'clock the next morning the coach pulled up at the door. The storm was over, but not the wind. The cold was intense. My team soon came up, but their ears and noses were badly frost bitten and otherwise showed the effects of the storm. I followed the coach but for a short distance only, as the snow which was drifting badly obliterated the trail. The six black horses on the coach were too much for my two bays and soon left me far in the rear. My compass had been lost and by noon I was back at the ranch I had previously left, the horses having made nearly a complete circle without my knowledge. I secured another compass and at nine o'clock that evening rolled into La Port, a city of adobe ranches, and stage station, where I put up for the night. (A place of two or three houses in those days was called a city.) I was informed that my chum was two miles up the river and in bad shape. The next morning I was up at day break. After grub I started and found my companion quartered in a little old log cabin at the base of the mountains, and being cared for by an aged squaw and her daughter—the old buck being out caring for the cattle. My chum had encountered the same kind of a storm as his rescuer, and unable to find his way was obliged to remain out the entire night and only one hundred feet from the cabin. Both of his feet were badly frozen. The Indians had done everything possible for him. The daughter, for an Indian, was extremely pretty, and I soon discovered that she was very much taken with my chum. I applied the remedies which I had brought. Then the little Indian maiden bundled him up, and with the promise that he would return they parted.

We were at once off on the return trip and arrived at the stage ranch, where I was cared for the previous night at just six o'clock. On driving up to the door of the station all three of the reaches of the buggy broke and gently dropped us to the ground. Fortunately there was a blacksmith connected with the station and I assisted him through the long night, forging reaches and repairing the buggy. At daylight we were off, reaching Denver in safety at 3:30 that afternoon and making the trip in just three days.

Both of my chum's feet had to be amputated at the insteps. He was very grateful and quite conscious of the fact that true friendship still existed.

Before leaving the governor's employ, I accompanied a mule train of ten wagons with supplies for the Ute tribe of Indians who lived in one of the parks of the mountains in the vicinity of Pike's Peak. The Utes, at that particular time, were on friendly terms with the white men as there was a treaty of peace existing between them and the Government.

CHAPTER V

A PROOF OF MARKSMANSHIP

We took with us a Mr. Baker, who was conceded to be one of the best guides, hunters, trappers and interpreters of that day, with a heart as large as an American bison, and as tender as a child's. But when his anger was aroused by danger or treachery, the very devil seemed to possess him; he had the courage of a lion, and was a dead shot. We had been friends for a long time, and on more than one occasion he had proved a true one.

The park was an ideal summer resort, an extended plateau with acres of fresh green grass, wild flowers, and virgin soil. In the center was a beautiful lake, its ice cold water well stocked with the finny tribe of speckled mountain trout, the delight of the angler. The park was inclosed by mountains of great height and grandeur, their rocky slopes were dotted with spruce, pine, and cottonwood, and capped with ages of crystal snow, presenting a sight more pleasing to the eye than the Falls of Niagara, and a perfect haven for an Indian maiden's love dream.

We had been in camp but a few days when Mr. Baker informed me that the young bucks, as the men of the tribe were called, wanted us to join in shooting at a target. After Mr. Baker and myself had made a few bull's eyes, they proposed we two should choose sides, and we did so. The teams were very evenly matched, making the game interesting. In the meantime, I had been presented to the chief in true Indian fashion and in turn was made known by him to his squaw, young bucks and maidens. The Indians had their tribal laws and customs as well as the white man and were required to live up to them. The maidens were two in number, their ages fourteen and seventeen moons respectively; the latter a picture of Indian beauty, perfect in every feature, form and carriage, a rare model for an artist. They were nearly always found together. At first they were quite reserved, but finally we became fast friends; we would ramble, hunt, fish from canoes and sail the placid waters of the little lake.

Early on the morning of the tenth day Mr. Baker entered my tent with a troubled look. I bade him good-morning and inquired the cause. Without fencing, he asked me if I wanted to be a squaw man. I asked him what the devil he was getting at.

AN OFFER OF MATRIMONY

He replied, "All there is to it, the old chief has taken a great liking to you, and wants you to marry Weenouah, his oldest daughter. He has plenty of money, and his horses and cattle run into four figures."

"That is no inducement," I said, "and it could never be."

Mr. Baker asked, "How are you going to get out of it?"

I replied, "I have been in lots of tight places, as you know, and have always managed to squeeze through, and I'll get out of this one in some way."

Little did either of us dream at that time of the manner, or rather the sacrifice, that one of us was doomed to bear, for me to escape the wrath of the old chief, when informed I would not marry his daughter. Fate decreed he was never to be so informed, but instead, a most cruel and unfortunate accident was to provide the means.

That afternoon the young bucks were again anxious to test their skill at the target. We all used the same carbine, which contained seven cartridges, one in the gun barrel and six in a magazine in the butt of the gun. Mr. Baker and I always tossed up a pebble to see who had first shot. As Mr. Baker won the first chance, he took aim and pulled the trigger and such an explosion as took place will never be forgotten. Everyone was stunned by its force. When the smoke had cleared, poor Baker's body was found lying on the ground with the lower jaw torn from its place. On recovering from the shock the young bucks fairly flew for the Indian medicine man. I quickly reached the corral and informed the wagon boss of the accident. He at once ordered the mules brought up. The light wagon was supplied with straw, blankets, commissary bottle and grub. Six of the fastest mules were hitched to the wagon and selecting two of the mulewhackers gave instruction for his care en route. I took the lines and quickly drove to the spot where poor Baker had fallen. Just as soon as the flow of blood had been checked and his wounds dressed we raised him gently and placed him in the wagon. Without a word I mounted the

63

driver's box and drove for all there was in those six mules, reaching Denver late the following night. Some who read this narrative may be skeptical, but it is a fact, nevertheless, that poor Baker recovered for I saw him a year later, but he could partake of liquid food only. The once stalwart form of that brave man, now emaciated and wasted to a mere skeleton, still stood erect.

THE TOLL OF THE PLAINS

My whole heart went out to him who, in years past, had hunted the antelope, deer, elk and buffalo; fought the cowardly savages and desperadoes on the thirsty plains and amidst the ragged slopes of the Rocky Mountains; penetrated the silent recesses of the dismal canyons and caves; crossed the snow covered divides; faced danger of every conceivable nature; and at last, although maimed for life, was grateful that he had escaped death and thankful in the thought that he had done his share in the settlement of the then Far West. As I gazed into his once keen eyes and beheld that shriveled face, my heart wrung with remorse, for I knew he had keenly suffered. Tears filled my eyes and trickled down my weather-beaten and sun-tanned boyish face, and I knew he accepted it as an emblem of my sorrow for being the innocent cause, in a measure, of his cruel misfortune. Thus, by the flip of a pebble was my life spared, but at the expense of a true friend.

CHAPTER VI

ON TO LEAVENWORTH

The next summer I was not very well, and so I made a trip to Leavenworth, Kansas, by the Southern or Smoky Hill route. We made the trip by mule train of twenty wagons with six mules hitched to each. The driver rode the nigh mule and with one line guided the team. If he wanted the leaders to go to the right he simply jerked fast or slow, depending on how quick he wanted to make the turn; if to the left, a steady or quick pull. The Indians on this trail were more numerous than on the Platte and scarcely a day passed that they were not to be seen, and continually trying to drive off our stock. We did not receive any great scare until we reached the Big Blue River where on the fourth day of July at ten o'clock in the morning a large Concord coach filled with passengers and a small guard of the United States soldiers, which had previously passed us, were awaiting our arrival before daring to proceed. On reaching the crest of the bluff leading to the valley of the river we saw hundreds of Sioux Indians, in war paint and feathers, camped on the opposite side in the underbrush and woods, and in the main trail directly in our path.

We at once went into corral. Thirty men against a horde of savages, if they were there to dispute our right of progress, was not a pleasant position to be placed in nor a fitting manner in which to celebrate the glorious Fourth. Consultations were numerous and all took part. The redskins, camped in plain sight, were hurrying to and fro, evidently in council like ourselves. To the right of the trail was a dense wood close to the river bank; on the left was a high perpendicular bluff, its sides unscalable, so our route was a genuine death trap, should they attack us. After grub all gathered in a circle and with pipes we proceeded with our last council. The situation was talked over from every point as to what the Indians might do or might not do. We finally arrived to the conclusion that they had the best of us whatever move we made. A majority vote decided to proceed with every man for himself in case of attack. Our wagons were empty which was a little in our favor as we could go on a mule trot or gallop. The coach filled with passengers was placed in the lead; and, being the youngest of the party, they were considerate enough to let me follow, and I did so as closely as possible. On reaching the river bottom, the driver of the coach started his horses on a run and the lash was put to every mule. We were all yelling like demons and on our approach the Indians left the trail and took to the river, thinking that we were a hundred or more strong. All passed safely through that valley of what might have been a horrible massacre. The unearthly racket we made was undoubtedly our salvation, but we were not out of danger by any means and continued our flight until eleven P. M. when we went into corral for food and rest. At three A. M. we again struck the trail and it is well that we did, for those blood-thirsty redskins laid death and destruction in their wake and came very near overtaking us a day later. Arriving at Leavenworth, I boarded a Missouri River palace for St. Louis, thence to New Orleans.

A FALSE FRIEND

On returning to St. Louis, I met a Westerner that I knew only by sight, and by him was induced to remain over a few days and take in the city. I did and was scooped. On the third morning I went through my pockets and the bed, piece by piece, dumping its contents in the center of the room, but my roll was gone. At once I sought my friend, but he was nowhere to be found. Plain case of misplaced confidence. He had made a touch. In my desperation, I made a confident of the caretaker of the hotel register. Being of a sympathetic nature, he consoled me with an invitation to stimulate, which I did. Being without a trunk, I was informed on my arrival it was customary to pay as you enter; fortunately I had a meal to my credit. I was in good condition, having had sufficient victuals to last the day, after which I proceeded to the river front and here discovered a boat bound for Omaha. I boarded her, sought out the steward, and applied for a position. He replied that he did not want any help.

"Well, I suppose you will let a fellow work his way, won't you?"

His answer was "Get off this craft," and without further talk, in not a very gentlemanly manner he assisted me.

On landing, I was mad clear through, and made up my mind I was going on that boat, and I did go. Just before the gang plank was pulled in I walked on board, keeping a sharp lookout for the steward. After I had avoided him for an hour and just as I was on the point of congratulating myself, I bumped into him.

"You on board?"

"It looks very much as if I were in evidence."

He grabbed me by the coat collar and hustled me before the captain. I told a straight story, and he, being a man, told the steward to take me up to the kitchen and set me to work. He did, and had his revenge in seeing that it was nearly continuous. After supper I worked the dish racket until twelve o'clock. At three the next morning he awoke me out of a sound sleep and set me to cleaning the woodwork of the cabin. Another of my desirable duties was to wash and polish the silver, throwing the water over the sides of the boat.

AN ALERT STEWARD

After dinner of the second day I proceeded with the tin bucket to the side of the boat and overboard went its contents, including three silver spoons. The spoons had no sooner left the bucket than I felt something of great force come in contact with the seat of my trousers. For a moment I thought surely perpetual motion had been discovered. Turning I was face to face with that infernal steward. Nor did that end my troubles for during the entire trip that particular locality of my person was the target for that fellow's boot. With a terrible oath, he informed me that my landing would be reached about midnight a day later and was called Wood Pile Landing. A short time before reaching the place, I was hustled from my bunk by the steward and in no gentle manner forced to the bow of the boat. The night was pitch dark, and produced a decidedly lonesome feeling in the one that was to be put off at a Wood Pile on the edge of an immense forest and undoubtedly miles from a dwelling. As the boat reached the bank, not even waiting for the gang plank to be shoved out, the old sinner gave me a push and at the same time applied the now familiar boot. I reached the earth on all fours. My first thought was to present him with a rock, but I curbed my temper, for I had no idea of deserting the old ship.

In those days the boilers of the boats were fired with cord wood purchased of the planters and delivered on the bank of the river. All boats plying on the Missouri River at that time were flat bottom with paddle wheel at the stern. Two long heavy poles were carried at the bow and worked with a windlass, being used to raise the bow of the boat when becoming fast on a sand bar. The pilot was obliged to keep a continuous lookout for these bars, as the channel was treacherous and changed often.

On approaching the river bank one of the deck hands would jump off with the bow line and make fast to a stump or tree, then the stern line was thrown to him and similarly connected. Then the negro deck hands would proceed to carry on the wood on their bare shoulders to the tune of a Southern plantation melody. When ready to start the bow line was cast off, the paddle wheel was started by the engine, and by means of the steering gear the craft was swung out into the stream, then the stern line was thrown aship, and the boat was off—but not without the steward's victim. No sooner had the colored gentlemen reached the deck, than I followed. Waiting until all was quiet aboard, I sought my berth. The next morning I proceeded with my work as if nothing had happened. I anticipated the steward's next move would be to throw me overboard, and in that belief told the cook of what he had done the previous night. At that point he came in, and on discovering me said, "You here again," his face purple with rage. His right foot at once became restless, he made a rush for me, but the cook with butcher-knife in hand prevented the action of said foot, and my troubles with that gentleman were over.

ARRIVAL AT LEAVENWORTH

We soon reached Leavenworth, and I left the boat without regret, but a much wiser youth. I went to the First National Bank of Leavenworth, drew my money, and after a few days' rest, I again embarked for Denver astride a mule. We saw plenty of Indians, but as the train was a long one they did not molest us.

On reaching the city of the plains I at once hunted up my old friend, the Major, who introduced me to the head of a firm of contractors, who were at that time engaged in getting out ties in the "Black Hills," for a portion of the Union Pacific railroad, then under construction. He told me that he wanted a man to go there and straighten out a set of books that a former employee had left badly mixed. He also took the trouble to inform me that the country was alive with Indians, and that the man who went there took big chances; and, if I were at all timid, I had better not accept the position. My friend gave me a strong recommend and I clinched the matter by telling the gentleman that I was not afraid of man, ghost or Indian.

He replied that I was just the man he was in search of, and would give me five hundred dollars in gold, a good horse and pay all expenses; that I should get my traps and be at the Planter's Hotel for dinner.

He expected his two partners from the east to inspect the camp and business, and everything was to be in readiness to depart on their arrival. Our conveyance was a full sized Concord coach with six good mules to draw it. The boot of the coach contained the best of everything to eat and drink—the latter being just as essential in that country as gun and ammunition. The partners were detained en route, and did not arrive until the second day, when they wished to rest and see the western sights, so we did not leave until the fourth day. Two Denverites accompanied us, making six in the party.

The first afternoon we made thirty-two miles, and camped near a stage station, where they keep, for the weary pilgrims, supplies and the rankest kind of corn juice known to the professional drinker.

The following morning we made an early start, and before noon rolled into La Port, on the Cachella Pondre River, the only settlement on the trail to the hills. We put up at the stage station for the night. There we met a drover, and a party of cow boys with one thousand head of California bronchos bound for the States. Those cowboys were as wild as western life could make them, yet, a jolly good lot.

During the evening, at the suggestion of someone, a poker game was started which lasted all night, and in the morning those who had indulged in the game were not feeling any too good—especially the losers—but,

71

nevertheless, they all strolled over to the large adobe corral to see our party off. Mr. A——, the head of the firm of contractors, had his large winnings safely concealed in a chamois bag placed close to his hide, where all wise men of the West carried their money in those days.

The drover had been a heavy but good loser. When about ready to hitch up our mules he called out to Mr. A——, "I'll go you six of my best bronchos against five hundred dollars that you haven't a man in your outfit that can drive the d——d brutes a mile and return."

The contractor approached me and asked if I thought I could do it. I told him that I was willing to take the chance.

Without another word he walked over to where the drover was standing and informed him that he would take the bet, provided he would have his cowpunchers hitch the little devils to the coach.

"Agreed," shouted the old fellow in no uncertain language.

The boys turned to the work with a will; for the fun expected, even if I received a broken neck for my daredevil recklessness, excited them to the highest pitch.

The reader has undoubtedly seen in the Wild West circuses the old-fashioned overland coach hung by heavy springs from front to rear axle. One of the most uncomfortable conveyances to ride in ever invented, especially for the driver, for, if the coach was not heavily loaded, when the front wheels dropped into a hole the old ramshackle thing was liable to topple over on the animals; and, if the driver was not securely strapped to the seat when the rear wheels reached the hole, he would land some distance in the rear. The contractor had the old ark properly balanced before starting, so I had no excuse to worry from that source.

The cowpunchers selected one broncho each and after a half hour's hawling, pulling and coaxing succeeded in hitching them to the coach. I climbed to the seat and was securely strapped with a large leather apron. Then I gathered up the lines and placed myself solidly for the start.

The whip socket contained a hickory stick five feet long with a lash twelve feet in length attached to one end. I gave the word to let them go, but the little bronchos thought different and balked. The number of times they bucked and threw themselves, started and bucked again, would be impossible to say. Finally the contractor accused the drover of being in collusion with his cowpuncher in order to win the wager by holding the bronchos back and a volley of words of not very mild character ensued, after which the six cowboys, three on either side of the team, stood off six feet. The noise made by the cracking of their whips their everlasting yelping made the excitement stronger than before, and I was off on the wildest ride I ever took. A hurdle jumper would not stand much of a chance with one of those wild bronchos.

A DANGEROUS RIDE

It was a lovely June morning and the bracing air of Colorado made me feel as wild as the young animals that were fast wheeling me over the dangerous trail and possibly into a camp of hostile Indians. I gave no thought to danger for I was too busy keeping the fiery little beasts to the trail. They were going at breakneck speed with no sign of tiring, so I let them go enjoying the sport even more than they. My hat went flying with the wind, I looked back, but could not see the ranch. How far I had left it behind, or what distance I had covered, I knew not.

At last I came to myself and realized for the first time what terrible danger I was in. Slowly turning the team to the right, I began a circle, hardly perceptible at first, but finally again reaching the trail. On the return trip, I plied the long lash to the leading pair. They shot forward faster than ever, all steaming with foam and covered with lather. At a great distance to the south I could see a party of Indians riding in the same direction. This additional danger seemed fairly to intoxicate me and I plied the whip with all my strength. The corral loomed up and then the stage station. The others, with hands in their pockets and mouth agape, were holding their breath; and, as we wheeled past them, the cowboys lashing the bronchos, a mighty shout went up. I had won the wager and was the lion of the day.

We did not make a start until the following morning. We fastened the bronchos together and tied the leader to the rear of the coach, and thus resumed our journey to the hills, where we safely arrived two days later, but minus four of the treacherous brutes. At night we always picketed them with the mules and the four that were lost had pulled their picket irons and undoubtedly gone to join the much read of "wild horses of the plains."

The camp in the hills consisted of shanties for fifteen hundred men, saw mill, and outfit store. The latter included in its stock plenty of the best kind of liquor. Each man was allowed three drinks a day and no more.

I had the books straightened out in due time and one day the contractor discovered he would soon be out of flour, and the nearest point at which it could be purchased was La Port, seventy-five miles distant. The Indians were troublesome, and each man who was asked refused to go, with one exception. The contractor finally made me a tempting offer to accompany a driver of a six mule team. I accepted, and at break of day the next morning we started. My companion on that dangerous trip was a plucky son of the Emerald Isle. We camped that night on Lodge Pole Creek. On the opposite side was an adobe ranch, and an immense stockade owned by a Frenchman with a Sioux squaw for a wife.

In our hurried start we had forgotten our tobacco, and without it my companion seemed lost. After grub I mounted my horse, and crossed over the creek to procure some. On making my wants known, I was freely supplied with tobacco, and was also informed that before we arrived they had been fighting the Indians for some time; that one of the cowboys had an arm badly shattered; and that they feared another attack the next morning. I returned to camp and told my companion of our danger.

A WELCOME HAVEN

After giving the animals plenty of feed and rest, we again took the trail at 4:30 A. M. As the day dawned, with the aid of a field glass, I discovered Indians swooping down on the ranch with the stockade at breakneck speed, and others coming in our direction. I told Patrick to urge the mules to a gallop. He suspected the cause and did so at once. Over the rolling ground we flew until the sun was well up in the heavens, and as each hour passed the redskins gained on us, until at last they could be seen with the naked eye. The harsh and cruel war-whoop of those blood-thirsty savages echoed and re-echoed back from the distant hills, and over the desolate plains until men and beasts were crazed to desperation. The lash was put to the already tired mules, and we strained every nerve to reach the crest of the next knoll, hoping against hope for succor. On they came, their warwhoops for scalps and the white man's blood was now continuous. The long feared report of their rifles was at last heard; bullets pierced our canvas covered wagon. We made a last desperate effort and reached the summit of the bluff. Not a half a mile from its base was a large corral of white covered wagons. Down the incline we flew, looking neither to the right nor the left, and, on reaching the corral, both men and beasts fell into a heap exhausted.

The red devils rode to the top of the hill, and the warwhoop of anger they sent up rings in my ears at times to this very day.

That evening we again took the trail and made the remainder of the trip by night drives. Reaching La Port the third morning, we secured our load and after giving the animals a much needed rest we started on the return trip. The fourth morning we arrived at the ranch with the stockade. Three mornings after we reached the foot of the hills where the company had a log cabin for their hunters and trappers, who, with their trusty rifles, furnished antelope, deer and buffalo meat for their small army of employees. On entering, a sight met our gaze too revolting to pass from memory. Upon the earthy floor lay two of those sturdy and warm-hearted dwellers of the plains and rockies, cold in death, scalped and mutilated almost beyond recognition—a deed committed by those dastardly red fiends of the Far West. Both were friends of mine and with uncovered head, in the presence of that gritty son of old Ireland, I vowed vengeance.

"At least, Charlie," said Patrick, "Let's give them a decent burial and move on."

We did so, reaching camp that evening just as the sun, with its beautiful tints of carmine, was bidding plains and hills goodnight, as if in memory of those stalwart and brave men who made the settlement and civilization of the West possible.

CHAPTER VII

A PLUCKY GERMAN

Two weeks later a strapping six-foot German, who was in charge of another camp further down the line, came for a visit. Shortly after his arrival, he proposed that we should go hunting, to which I agreed.

That morning, as usual, the men called for their liquor, and among them was a long lanky fellow with red hair and bushy beard. He certainly had the appearance of an outlaw. He had received one glass of grog and came for the second which I refused him. Without a word I was on my back. At that point the German came in and caught him with the left hand in the same locality. Suffering with pain and crazed with liquor, he left the store, secured his revolvers and returned. I was behind the counter at the time with my back to the door. The first thing I knew I heard the report of a revolver and a bullet whizzed past my ear and buried itself in a can of tomatoes not six inches from my head. As I turned around, I saw the fellow being propelled through the door by the German's right. At that point the contractor came in and after being told of what had happened, he discharged the fellow. He wished to retain his revolvers, but his request was not granted. He had an old-fashioned army musket and begged to be allowed to keep that. I told Mr. A—— not to let him have it for I was satisfied from the blow he gave me that he was a bad actor; but Mr. A——, being good natured and kind hearted, consented. He ordered four days' rations put up for him and he left camp in an ugly mood and was given no further thought.

After grub, the German proposed that we flip a coin to see who should go for the horses. The visitor losing, he at once started for the canyon below where the horses were grazing. Shortly after I heard a shot and then many more, but gave it no heed as it was a common occurrence there. Half an hour later one of the men came in and told me that the German lay dead in the canyon below. I, with the others in camp, proceeded to the point indicated, where we found the poor fellow lying on his back. A bullet from that villain's musket had pierced his heart. His watch, belt of cartridges, revolvers, and repeating carbine were gone. After we returned with the body, Mr. A—— had the mill whistle blown calling all hands to quarters and for three days and nights with little sleep or rest we searched those hills and trails leading to Salt Lake and Denver. We picketed men on each trail to search all passing trains; but the demon gave us the slip, and cheated that maddened crowd of a lynching, or something worse; perhaps a tug of war between two wild bronchos, which we had in camp, with that man's body as the connecting link.

I can to this day remember just how that poor fellow looked; cold in death, far from home and loved ones, with no mother to weep at his bier. With uncovered heads we lowered him in earth, in a rough box, at the foot of one of the tall sentinels of the hills, and placed a slab to mark the spot, that his friends might some day claim all that remained of as brave and honest a German as ever lived.

A WATCHFUL PROVIDENCE

Thus by the toss of a coin was my life again spared. This last narrow escape from death was the fourteenth of which I positively knew, and how many more that I did not know of, it is impossible to tell; so I made up my mind to get out of the country alive, if possible. I informed Mr. A—— of my intentions and the following day closed my business and at dusk that evening I started, unaccompanied, on a two hundred mile ride over a trail watched by hundreds of blood-thirsty Indians. I knew that no Indian pony could overtake my fleet runner, and all that was to be feared was a surprise or have my horse shot from under me. I camped far from the trail, with lariat fastened to my wrist, never closing my eyes until my faithful animal had laid down for the day. His first move at dusk awoke me, and, after feed, we were off with the wind at breakneck speed.

At the close of the second day, while I lay sleeping on the desert sands with the saddle blanket for a pillow, and dreaming of my far away home, it seemed as if something of a slimy nature was slowly crawling over the calf of my bare leg. On gaining partial consciousness, too quickly did I realize that it was a reality and not a dream. A rattlesnake's long slimy body was crossing that bridge of flesh, squirming along for a couple of inches, then raising its repulsive body a foot or more and turning its insignificant head, would look straight towards my partly closed eyes and, with its hideous mouth agape, would dart its poisonous arrow-like tongue in and out like lightning, then lowering itself, it would resume the same tactics as before. How many times it repeated this, I shall never know. No words have ever been formed that can adequately express the feeling that took possession of me. I seemed powerless to move a muscle or twitch an eyelid. The suspense was terrible, expecting each time that the slimy body descended the viper would thrust his poisonous lance into my leg and all would be over. The horror of it all cannot be imagined, and to this day, when I recall the incident, it sends a shiver through my entire body. As the coarse rattles of his tail left the bare flesh of my leg, my senses seemed to return; but it was only for a moment, for through the pant of my right leg I felt that same crawling sensation and I knew in an instant that it was a mate following the one that had just passed over the bridge of flesh. As soon as it reached the bare leg the dirty reptile went through the same horrible stunts as the first one. The agony seemed impossible to bear and when at last the thing had completed its journey and was at a safe distance away, I leaped into the air—how far I shall leave the reader to surmise. Crazed with anger and trembling from head to foot, I rushed for my revolvers and fired at random. I was considered a good shot in those days, but in this excited condition I would not have been able to hit a barn. I ran for my Henry Carbine and, grasping it by the barrel, made short work of ridding the earth of the cause that had produced the most terrifying scare experience during my western life.

THE FAITHFUL HORSE

For the first time during the excitement my thoughts turned to my faithful horse, but he was nowhere to be seen. The horror of the situation began to dawn upon me and I realized at once that I was lost on that desolate plain—one hundred miles from any camp that I knew of and apparently alone. I cried out, "My God, what can be done!" The thought was enough to drive one crazy. Can I ever forget it? I think not; nor could anyone. Even to see or talk to an Indian would have been a comfort. Driven to agonizing despair I ran for my field glass and scanned the rolling ground in every direction. Buffalo, deer, antelope, coyote, and a small party of horsemen were visible, but the latter too far away to make out if they were United States Cavalrymen or Indians. Looking again, without my glass, I discovered my horse standing on a high knoll not more than a half mile away with head and tail erect; the breath from his dilated nostrils ascending heavenward in the cold October air and presenting a picture for an artist. I called loudly, "Billie, Billie," and with outstretched hand walked slowly toward him, but he looked not in my direction. All of a sudden he made a quick bound and was off. My heart seemed to stop beating. A minute seemed an hour; but I kept walking after him and he finally stopped, turned around and faced me. That look can never be forgotten. With ears thrown back, he came slowly toward me. Again, I called "Billie, Billie," and held out both hands and with a whinner he came on a gallop, trembling in every muscle, seemingly as frightened as myself. I patted his neck, straightened out his rich heavy mane, rubbed his face and nose and kissed him. He licked my cheek and hand in appreciation of my welcome; moisture gathered in his large eyes and I cried with joy—like a child that I was—and then we both felt better. I coiled up the lariat and placed my right arm over his perfectly formed neck and slowly walked to our little camp. I rubbed him down until he was perfectly dry; then curried, brushed and rubbed until I could almost see myself in his coat of silky hair. Then I made him lay down and did the same thing myself, using his withers and mane for a pillow. When I awoke the moon shown full in our faces. I patted his neck and soon those large eyes were looking affectionately into mine. I sprang to my feet and he did the same. After brushing off the side on which he had laid, I placed the saddle blanket, buckled taut the saddle, gathered up my small camp kit and fastened it to the rear of the saddle, coiled the lariat and hung it on the pommel of the saddle, fastened on my spurs—from which he had never felt even the slightest touch—threw my field glass over my left shoulder, buckled on my cartridge belt and revolvers, swung my canteen and Henry Carbine over my right shoulder, and with a leap, landed astride the saddle, and was off with the wind in search of the trail two full miles away.

THE INDIANS CAPTURE A FRIEND

Early on the morning of the third day, I stopped at a stage station, where I met the assistant wagon boss who was with the bull train during my first trip across the plains. He was a genuine Missouri Bushwacker and a desperate fellow. Like all others of his class he wore his hair long, making it a much coveted prize for the Indians. After the day's visit and relating our experience of western life, he told me that he was on his way to the Black Hills. I reluctantly volunteered the information to him that I did not think he would ever reach there on the old skate he was riding, and that he should not venture on the trail until after dark, but he knew it all and started at sundown. I was sure the fellow would never reach the Hills, nor was I mistaken, for in less than an hour the Salt Lake Coach rolled up to the door of the station, and the driver asked if a horseman had put up at the place, and being informed that there had, told us the Indians had captured him and tied him to one of their own ponies and was rapidly going north, leaving his old nag to be picked up by any one who would care for it. Not a day passed that the unwelcome savages were not to be seen, and we were chased many times, but the faithful animal reached Denver in safety.

The Union Pacific railroad had then reached Julesburg and I conceived the hazardous idea of reaching that point by navigating the Platte River—a distance of three hundred miles—so I at once ordered a flat bottomed boat built of material in the rough.

A CUNNING SCHEMER

I next went in quest of my aged chum, the ex-pig dealer, who, when found, revealed by a twinkle in his eye another dare-devil scheme, which he was quite capable of concocting when alone in his warehouse den. He exclaimed, with much feeling and a forced tear, that he was right down glad to see me safely back and gave me little rest until I had related my experiences in the hills. He then unfolded his diabolical scheme, whereby both of us could lay a foundation for a fortune. I was in need of the latter, without any question, but not by this method.

Cheyenne had just been surveyed, mapped and laid out, and the proposition was for him to furnish a man, two mule teams, wagons, tents, provisions and all other necessities; and this man and myself were to go there and squat or take possession of two sections of Government land, consisting of one hundred and sixty acres each, located just outside the city limits. The offer was promptly rejected, and it destroyed the last particle of friendship that had existed between us as far as I was concerned. I had just been through that part of the country and had narrowly escaped death many times, and for us to carry out this scheme, I knew would be impossible, for the tricky redskins would be certain to capture us. I cannot recollect the exact reply that I made him, but am positive I requested him to go to Hades by the shortest possible route. We parted in anger after three long years of friendship. The old major's love for the almighty dollar was the cause. I never did have a very strong desire to furnish material to the cruel savages for one of their home scalp dances, and besides my mind was made up to leave Colorado, which I did.

I afterwards made the acquaintance of a young fellow, a college graduate who had been unable to secure a position to his liking and was anxious to return to the States. After a few days of good fellowship, and finding him of the right material, I made my plans known to him. He at once fell in with them, and a week later we embarked on our perilous journey. We started at full moon drifting with a comparatively strong current using paddles to guide our roughly constructed craft. We made nightly rides of about fifty miles, and at dawn would land on one of the small islands of the river, conceal ourselves and the boat in the tall grass from which we were able to see all that passed by trail and bluffs, and not be seen ourselves. Our greatest danger was in being discovered by the Indians on the high bluffs, or a visit from them to the island we occupied. The first scare we had was when a party of a dozen or more rode to the bank of the river for the purpose, as we supposed, of crossing. They seemed, however, undecided as to their course, but finally urged their ponies down the bank and into the river. To describe our feelings would be impossible. Just then, to us, a minute seemed an hour. Cold beads of perspiration stood out on both, not exactly from fear, but a sort of yearning to be elsewhere; and I wondered, after all that I had passed through, if I was to be cut down on my homeward journey by those fiendish red devils. "Saved!" whispered my friend, "they are leaving the river." And sure enough those little prairie ponies were climbing the bank on a dead run for the bluffs.

HOME RIDE DOWN THE PLATTE RIVER

The last night of that eventful ride lasted long until after the sun was up. The large Concord coach filled with passengers passed close to the river bank a short time before, and from the driver we learned we were ten miles from Julesburg. We proceeded, keeping close to the bank, and with field glass continually swept the valley and bluffs in every direction. We were facing a mild and depressing wind. All of a sudden dismal sounds reached our ears, and as the noiseless current of the river rounded the projecting points in its banks, it bore our staunch old craft to a place of safety, or ourselves to a cruel death, we knew not which. The sounds became more distinct until both of us were satisfied that the Indians had captured the overland coach with its load of human freight. As we rounded the next bend the river took a straight course, but there was no island in sight.

"No island in sight," said my friend. "Where can we go?" And turning around I discovered he was as white as a sheet. As for myself, I was hanging to the edge of the bank trying hard to collect my wits and recover from a fainting spell. We finally managed to get the boat back and around the bend where we lay concealed for some time, suffering the torture of Hades. I finally crawled to the top of the bank and with field glass surveyed the locality in every direction. No life was visible, still the unearthly noise kept up, and the feeling of those two lone travelers would be impossible to describe. The thought at last came to me that we must be somewhere in the vicinity of the old California Crossing. I crawled back to the boat and told my companion to go ahead, while I continually used the field glass. After fifteen minutes, I discovered a white speck in the eastern horizon. We were soon over our fright, and with light hearts were sailing over the rippling waters of the old Platte feeling assured that we would soon reach a place of safety, as far as the Indians were concerned.

On arriving at the crossing, which it proved to be, we found one of those large white covered prairie schooners stalled in the middle of the stream, and fifty Greasers, as the Mexican drivers were called, and as many yoke of oxen trying to haul it out.

FAREWELL TO THE PLAINS

We sailed merrily along and at two P. M. reached Julesburg, the then terminus of the Union Pacific railroad and overland shipping point for all territory west, north and south. The Union Pacific railroad, when under construction, made a terminus every two or three hundred miles. The houses were built in sections, so they were easily taken apart, loaded on flat freight cars, and taken to the next terminus completely deserting the former town, Julesburg was rightfully named "The Portable Hell of the Plains." My finer feelings cannot, if words could, attempt a description. Suffice to say that during the three days we were there four men and women were buried in their street costumes. The fourth day we boarded a Union Pacific train and were whirled to its Eastern terminus, Omaha, thence home, arriving safely after an absence of four years.

The habits formed during those western years were hard to change, and the fight of my life to live a semblance of the proper life, required a will power as irresistible as the crystal quartz taken from the lofty snow capped mountain sides, taking tons of weight to crush it, that the good might be separated from the worthless.

BOOK TWO

DAYS ON THE ROAD

CROSSING THE PLAINS IN 1865

BY
SARAH RAYMOND HERNDON

NEW YORK
BURR PRINTING HOUSE

PREFACE.

I do not expect to gain fame or fortune by the publication of this little book. I have prepared it for publication, because a number of the pioneers who read my journal twenty years ago, when published in *The Husbandman*, have asked me to.

At that time I was a busy wife, mother and housekeeper, and could only write when my baby boy was taking his daily nap, to supply the copy for each week. No one knows better than I how very imperfect it was, yet many seemed to enjoy it, and the press that noticed it at all spoke very kindly of it.

S. R. H.

DEDICATED TO

THE PIONEERS OF MONTANA AND THE "GREAT WEST,"
WHO CROSSED THE PLAINS IN WAGONS.

REMINISCENCES OF THE PLAINS

BY DR. HOWARD.

Editor *Husbandman.*—Through your kindness to Mrs. Howard, we are a reader of your excellent journal. Hence a few months ago our eyes fell upon "Reminisences of Pilgrimage Across the Plains in 1865," by S. R. H., and at once recognized the writer as the "lady who rode the gallant bay." And now, sir, as we were an humble member of the gallant McMahan train, frequently referred to in her interesting journal, permit me through the columns of your paper to tender her the thanks and gratitude, not only of ourselves, but every surviving member of that train, for affording us the pleasure of again traveling that eventful road without the fatigue and hardships of a long and tiresome journey. And even now, after the lapse of fifteen years, to be so pleasantly reminded of our "Gallant Bearing" and the confidence reposed in us for protection, while passing through the Indian country, we almost regret that the savages did not give us a striking opportunity of displaying our prowess. It was our pleasure to form the acquaintance of the writer, as correctly stated, on the north bank of the South Platte, near the foot of Fremont's Orchard. The present editor of the *Husbandman*, then a beardless youth, had been suffering with typho-malarial fever from the time we left Nebraska City, and we visited her camp (ostensibly) begging bread, and obtained as good as was ever baked upon the plains. From this time on, at least for some hundreds of miles, it was our pleasure to meet her on the road and in camp. We were in different trains, but camped near each other every night for protection from the Indians. Very soon, somehow or other, when our trains were preparing to drive out every morning, and Miss R. was mounting Dick, we were in the act of mounting our pony Jo, and even at this day, in thinking over the matter, I am induced to believe that our ponies became somewhat attached to each other, as they would instinctively fall into each other's company. This was the state of affairs existing at Elk Mountain, where the bouquet was gathered and presented, and where, it is frankly admitted, we became somewhat partial.

Well, we do recollect the crossing of North Platte, that turbulent stream on the Fort Halleck route. Train after train was crossing all day long. We were standing on the bank, with Captain McMahan, when the Hardinbrooke train, the one in which she was traveling, approached the crossing, and we discovered Miss Raymond on the front seat of the wagon, with lines in hand, in the attitude of driving. We remarked, "Good gracious, look yonder, is it possible Miss Raymond is going to drive that team across this terrible stream alone?"

"Now," said Captain McMahan, "is the time to show your gallantry."

And before we could think twice, she drove bravely in. Of course we mounted Jo and followed after her, and here on a little island in the middle of the river is where we rode up and congratulated her on her skill as a driver. As we approached the place of our destination our trains became separated. Miss R. preceded us a few days to the Golden City. It was our pleasure, however, to visit her in the little domicile mentioned in her narrative, and

Talk our troubles over, our journey through at last,
And in her happy presence we forgot the gloomy past.

We sojourned in Virginia City but a short time, then crossed a tributary of the Missouri near their confluence, and wintered at Diamond City Confederate Gulch. The June following we returned to our native State.

A year after our return Captain McMahan and myself received cards announcing the nuptials of Miss Raymond and Mr. Herndon, which cards now occupy receivers on our center tables, for which we were ever thankful, and at which time, of course, the bouquet crumbled to dust. And now wishing the "lady who rode the gallant bay" and the lucky gentleman whose home she makes happy, long life and the enjoyment of a Montana home; I am,

Truly yours,
W. HOWARD.

DAYS ON THE ROAD

Mrs. Delilah Raymond (widow) and her children
Sarah (Sallie), William Hillhouse, and Winthrop
began their westward journey on May 1, 1865. This
diary was written by Sarah.

Sarah Raymond Herndon

WE START.

As I sit here in the shade of our prairie-schooner, with this blank book ready to record the events of this our first day on the road, the thought comes to me:

"Why are we here? Why have we left home, friends, relatives, associates, and loved ones, who have made so large a part of our lives and added so much to our happiness?"

"Echo answers 'Why?'"

"The chief aim in life is the pursuit of life, liberty, and happiness." Are we not taking great risks, in thus venturing into the wilderness? When devoted men and women leave home, friends and the enjoyments of life to go to some far heathen land, obeying the command: "Go, preach my Gospel, to every creature," we look on and applaud and desire to emulate them. There is something so sublime, so noble in the act that elevates the missionary above the common order of human beings that we are not surprised that they make the sacrifice, and we silently wish that we, too, had been called to do missionary work.

But when people who are comfortably and pleasantly situated pull up stakes and leave all, or nearly all, that makes life worth the living, start on a long, tedious, and perhaps dangerous journey, to seek a home in a strange land among strangers, with no other motive than that of bettering their circumstances, by gaining wealth, and heaping together riches, that perish with the using, it does seem strange that so many people do it.

The motive does not seem to justify the inconvenience, the anxiety, the suspense that must be endured. Yet how would the great West be peopled were it not so? God knows best. It is, without doubt, this spirit of restlessness, and unsatisfied longing, or ambition—if you please—which is implanted in our nature by an all-wise Creator that has peopled the whole earth.

This has been a glorious May-day. The sky most beautifully blue, the atmosphere delightfully pure, the birds twittering joyously, the earth seems filled with joy and gladness. God has given us this auspicious day to inspire our hearts with hope and joyful anticipation, this our first day's journey on the road across the plains and mountains.

It was hard to say good-bye to our loved and loving friends, knowing that we were not at all likely to meet again in this life. I felt very much like indulging in a good cry, but refrained, and Dick and I were soon speeding over the beautiful prairie, overtaking Cash, who had lingered behind the others, waiting for me.

"A penny for your thoughts, Cash?"

"I was wondering if we will ever tread Missouri soil again?"

"Quite likely we shall, we are young in years, with a long life before us, no doubt we will come on a visit to Missouri when we get rich."

We were passing a very comfortable looking farmhouse, men, women, and children were in the yard, gazing after us, as we cantered past.

"Don't you believe they envy us and wish they were going, too?"

"No, why should they?"

"Oh, because it is so jolly to be going across the continent; it is like a picnic every day for months; I was always sorry picnic days were so short, and now it will be an all Summer picnic."

"I wish I felt that way; aren't you sorry to leave your friends?"

"Of course I am, but then I shall write long letters to them, and they will write to me, and I will make new friends wherever I go, and somehow I am glad I am going."

After we came within sight of our caravan we walked our ponies, and talked of many things, past, present, and future. When within a mile or two of Memphis our first camp was made. Our six wagons, with their snow-white covers, and Mr. Kerfoot's big tent, make a very respectable looking camp.

OUR FIRST CAMP.

As we were provided with fresh bread, cake, cold chicken, boiled ham, pickles, preserves, etc., supper was quickly prepared for our small family of four, and we enjoyed it immensely. Then comes my time to write, as I have promised friends that I will keep a journal on this trip. Mr. Kerfoot thinks the Government is going to smash and green-backs will not be worth one cent on the dollar, so he has turned all his money into gold coin, and stowed it into a small leather satchel—it seems quite heavy to lift or carry.

As Mrs. Kerfoot was sitting on a camp-chair near our wagons, Mr. Kerfoot came toward her, saying, "Here, mother, I want you to take care of this satchel, it is all we will ask you to do, the girls will cook and wash dishes, the boys take care of the stock, and I will oversee things generally, and we will do nicely." She accepted the responsibility without a word, and as he walked away she turned to me, and said, "I wish it was in some good bank, I expect nothing else but that it will be stolen, and then what will become of us?"

While I have been writing Neelie (Cornelia) and Sittie (Henrietta) have been getting supper for a family of twelve, no small undertaking for them, as they have been used to servants and know very little about cooking.

When everything was ready, Neelie came to her mother exclaiming, "Come, mamma, to supper, the first ever prepared by your own little girl, but not the last I hope, see how nicely the table looks, Emma and Delia picked those wild flowers for you, how brightly the new tinware shines, let us imagine it is silver and it will answer the same purpose as if it were."

Her mother smiles cheerfully, as she takes her arm, Cash sneers at Neelie's nonsense—as she calls it. Mr. Kerfoot nods approval, as Neelie escorts her mother to the table. When all are seated Mr. Kerfoot bows his head and asks God's blessing on the meal.

Every one seems to enjoy this picnic style of taking supper out of doors, and linger so long at the table, that

Neelie has to hint that other work will have to be done before dark.

When at last the table is cleared, she says to Emma and Delia, "Don't you want to help me wash these nice, bright dishes and put them away?"

They are always ready to help Neelie, and the work is soon done. Amid laughter and fun they hardly realize they have been at work. Mr. Kerfoot insists that we women and the children must sleep in houses as long as there are houses to sleep in. Mother and I would greatly prefer sleeping in our spring-wagon, to making a bed on the floor in a room with so many, but as he has hired the room we do not want to seem contrary, so have offered no objection. The boys have carried the mattresses and bedding into the house, and Neelie has come for me to go with her to arrange our sleeping-room. So good-night.

THROUGH MEMPHIS.

May 2.

We were up with the sun this morning after a night of refreshing and restful sleep. Neelie and I commenced folding the bedclothes, ready to be sent to the wagons, when she startled me with a merry peal of laughter, "Look here, Miss Sallie, see ma's treasure, she has left it on the floor under the head of her bed. Don't say anything, and I will put it in the bottom of a trunk, where it ought to be, and we will see how long it will be before she misses it."

She thought of it while at breakfast, and started up excitedly, "Neelie daughter, did you see that precious satchel?"

"Yes, ma, I have taken care of it, and put it where it will not be left lying around loose any more."

"Thank you, my dear, I am glad you have taken care of it."

"Why, mother, I did not expect you to carry that burden around on your arm by day, and sleep with it at night. I only intend for you to have entire charge of it, and put it where the rest of us do not know the hiding place, so that when we are obliged to have some, we will have to come to you to get it. And then give it sparingly, for much, very much depends upon what is in that satchel."

I MEET AN ACQUAINTANCE.

We came to Memphis about nine A.M. Court is in session, several friends and acquaintances, who are attending court, came to the wagons to say good-bye. Mother's brother, Uncle Zack, was among them, he said, "Remember, when you wish yourselves back here, that *I* told you not to go."

"Yes, we will when that times comes and send you a vote of thanks for your good advice," I replied.

Cash, Neelie and I have been riding our ponies all day. We are stopping in a beautiful place for camping, near the farmhouse of a Mr. and Mrs. Fifer. They are very pleasant elderly people, who have raised a family of six children, who are all married, and gone to homes of their own. It is a delightfully homey home, yet it seems sad that they should be left alone in their old age. We will sleep in the house again to-night, I shall be glad when we get to where there are no houses to sleep in, for it does not seem like camping out when we sleep in houses. Cash and Neelie want to sleep in the tent, but their father says no, and his word is law in this camp.

*   *   *   *   *

Wednesday, May 3.

Brother Hillhouse discovered very early this morning that the tire on one of the wheels of the ox-wagon was broken. He started off ahead of the rest of the wagons to find a blacksmith shop and get it mended by the time we would overtake him. It was ten o'clock when we came to the shop, near a flour-mill. There was a very bad piece of road before we crossed the creek, a deep ditch had been washed out by the Spring rains. I waited to see the wagons safely over, when some one came beside my pony with outstretched hand saying, "Good-morning, Miss Raymond, I see you are in earnest about crossing the plains."

"Why, how do you do, Mr. Smith? Am glad to see you, of course I am in earnest about crossing the plains, but where did you come from? I supposed you would be at the Missouri River before this time, have you turned back?"

"Oh, no, we are waiting for better roads and good company."

"Come, go with us, I will promise you good company, and the roads will improve."

"Where are Cash and Neelie? I have not seen them."

"They did not stop, when I waited to see the wagons over the difficulties."

"Then I have missed seeing them; was in the mill when they passed. Remember me to them. We will start again to-morrow, and will overtake you in a few days, perhaps."

"Hope you will, good-bye until we meet again."

"Farewell, may you enjoy as pleasant a trip as you anticipate."

"Thank you," and waving him good-bye, I spoke to Dick, and he cantered up the hill past the mill and the wagons. I soon caught up with Cash and Neelie.

"Guess who I saw at the mill?"

"Did you see any one we know?"

"Yes, an especial friend of yours, Cash, Bob Smith, of Liberty."

"Oh, dear, I wish I had seen him. Was Thad Harper with him? Are they going back home?"

"No; they are waiting for better roads and good company. I did not see Thad Harper. Bob said they will overtake us in a few days."

"I hope they will, they would be quite an addition to our party."

AN ADDITION TO OUR PARTY.

"Yes, but they won't; do you suppose they are going to let us see them cooking and washing dishes? Not if they know themselves. Then they would have to play the agreeable once in a while, and that is what they are not going to do on a trip of this kind. I do not expect to see them, they would rather stay where they are another week than join our party."

"I believe you are right, Neelie, for he did not say good-bye as if he expected to see me very soon."

When it was time to stop for lunch, we found a very nice place and waited for the wagons. While at lunch we saw an emigrant wagon, drawn by three yoke of oxen, coming up the road, and were somewhat surprised to see it turn from the road and come toward our camp. It proved to be Mr. John Milburn, of Etna, and his sister Augusta. They have traveled in one day and a half the distance we have been two and a half days coming.

Miss Milburn is a very intelligent, well-educated young lady, some two or three years my senior. We are not very well acquainted with her, but have met her frequently, and have known of her several years. She is an active member of the Presbyterian Church at Etna. She has her little nephew, Ernest Talbot, with her. He is seven years old, her sister's dying gift, a very bright child and considerably spoiled, but dear to his auntie's heart as her own life. They have started to Montana to get rich in the gold mines. Mr. Milburn leaves a wife and two small children with his widowed mother, to watch, and wait, and pray for his success and safe return home.

We crossed the dividing line—though we did not see it—between Missouri and Iowa soon after noon, and it is very probable some of us will never tread Missouri soil again. As we were coming through Stilesville, a small town this side the line, there were several loafers in front of a saloon who acted very rudely, to say the least.

We distinctly heard such remarks as the following, "Whew, what pretty girls, and how well they ride—Missourians I'll bet."

"Say, boys, let's try our luck; maybe we can each hook a pony to-night?"

Mr. Milburn's team is so tired out with such fast driving that we have stopped earlier than usual, and I have had more time to write. We are only two or three miles from Stilesville. The weather is perfect; we will sleep in the wagons to-night. Mr. Kerfoot thinks it necessary to guard the camp. I believe it an unnecessary precaution, for if those loafers at Stilesville had meant mischief they would not have expressed themselves so freely. However, Ezra and Frank Kerfoot (Mr. Kerfoot's nephews), Sim Buford, and Brother Hillhouse, will take turns standing guard, each one for two hours.

*   *   *   *   *

Thursday, May 4.

Oh, how we did sleep last night, dreamless and sound. Our first night in the wagons was undisturbed and sweet. We were up with the birds making ready for an early start. Mother prepares breakfast, while I roll up the beds and cover closely to protect them from the dust; one of the boys milks the cows, while I assist mother, and when breakfast of hot biscuit, ham and eggs, apple-sauce, coffee, and breakfast-food (which I should have mentioned first), is over, I strain the milk into an old-fashioned churn that is big at the bottom and little at the top, cover closely and fix it in the front of the freight wagon, where it will be churned by the motion of the wagon, and we have a pat of the sweetest, most delicious butter when we stop in the evening that any one ever tasted. Mother washes the dishes, we prepare lunch for our noon meal, I stow it in the grub-box under the seat in the spring-wagon, the boys take the pipe off the little sheet-iron stove, empty the fire out and leave it to cool, while I am putting things away in the places where they belong. It is wonderful how soon we have learned to live in a wagon, and we seem to have an abundance of room.

When horses are harnessed, oxen yoked—and everything ready to start, we girls proceed to saddle our ponies; some of the boys usually come and offer assistance, which is politely declined, as we are going to wait upon ourselves on this trip.

The wagons start, leaving us to follow at our leisure. We don our riding-habits, made of dark-brown denim, that completely cover, and protect us from mud and dust, tie on our sun-bonnets, mount our ponies unassisted, and soon overtake and pass the wagons.

We started this morning at seven o'clock. It is delightful riding horseback in the early morning.

BLOOMFIELD, IOWA.

We were on the lookout for Bloomfield, about ten o'clock we could see the spires and steeples glittering in the sunshine. When we reached the suburbs we stopped to wait for the wagons.

When we reached the business part of the city, I dismounted and made ready to do some shopping, as a few necessary articles had been forgotten when purchasing our outfit.

"Aren't you going with me, girls?"

"Oh, dear, no; not in these togs, short dresses, thick shoes, sun-bonnets, etc."

"I think we appear much better in our short dresses, thick shoes, and sun-bonnets than we would in trailing skirts, French kid shoes, and hats of the latest style, especially as we are emigrants, and not ladies at home. However, I do not wish you to suffer mortification on my account, some one of the boys will go with me."

"May I go, Miss Sallie?" Ezra asked.

"Certainly, and thank you to."

We called at two drug stores, one grocery and several dry-goods establishments, and made several small purchases. The clerks seemed quite interested, and asked numerous questions. Some wished they were going, too; others thought we had a long, hard journey before us.

When we came back, they were waiting for us. I gave the satchel containing the purchases into mother's care, mounted Dick, and we were soon on the way. About a mile from Bloomfield we stopped for lunch of sandwiches, ginger-bread, cheese, fruit and milk.

We all have such ravenous appetites, the plainest food is relished and enjoyed, as we never enjoyed food before. If any one suffering from loss of appetite, or insomnia, would take a trip of this kind, they would soon find their appetite, and sleep the night through without waking.

Brother Winthrop wanted to ride Dick this afternoon, so I took passage with mother and drove the horses until I began to nod, when I gave the lines to her and climbed back into the wagon for an afternoon nap. I waked up as we were driving into Drakesville, a small but very pretty town. Mother and I talked the rest of the afternoon, she enjoys this life as much as I do; we built air-castles for our future habitation; I trust there was not enough selfishness in the building material to hurt us if they tumble about our ears.

Mother seems happier than she has since the war commenced, and our eldest brother, Mac, went into the army. We stopped for the night earlier than usual, about five o'clock. We are camping in a lane near a farmhouse.

Our little sheet-iron stove is taken down from its place on a shelf at the back of the freight wagon. Mother gets dinner and prepares something for lunch to-morrow, at the same time. The boys buy feed from the farmers, as the grass is not long enough to satisfy the horses and cattle. I write as long as it is light enough to see.

The young people complain about my taking so much time to write, but since I have commenced I cannot stop. I am thinking all the time about what things are worth recording.

(A call to dinner.)

BEAUTIFUL APPLES.

After dinner mother washes the dishes and makes all the arrangements she can for an early breakfast. She thinks I am another "Harriet Beecher Stowe," so she is perfectly willing to do the work in the evening and let me write. Oh, the unselfishness of mothers. I do my share, of course, mornings, and at noon, but evenings I only make the beds in both wagons.

We have white sheets and pillow-cases, with a pair of blankets, and light comforts on both beds, just the same as at home, and they do not soil any more or any quicker, as we have them carefully protected from dust.

I had been writing a little while after dinner, when Frank stepped up with a basket of beautiful red-cheeked apples in his hand, not a wilted one among them.

"Where shall I put them?"

"Oh, Frank, how lovely they are. Where did you get them? Thank you so much; they are not *all* for me?"—as he emptied the last one into the pan. "Are all the others supplied? This seems more than my share."

"Yes; they are for you, we bought the farmer's entire stock; the others are supplied, or will be without you giving them yours."

He had just gone, when Sim Buford came and threw half a dozen especially beautiful ones into my lap.

"Thank you, Sim, but I am bountifully supplied, don't you see?"

"So you are, but keep mine, too; I can guess who it was that forestalled me." Laughing as he walked off.

So we are feasting on luscious apples this evening, thanks to the generosity of our young gentlemen.

*   *   *   *   *

Friday, May 5.

We came through Unionville and Moravia to-day. Have traveled farther and later than any day yet. It was almost dark when we stopped, and raining, too; to make a bad matter worse, we are camping in a disagreeable muddy place, and have to use lanterns to cook by.

We were obliged to come so far to get a lot large enough to hold the stock. We will be glad to sleep in the house to-night.

Mrs. Kerfoot is homesick, blue and despondent this evening; she has always had such an easy life that anything disagreeable discourages her. Perhaps when the sun shines again she will feel all right.

*   *   *   *   *

Saturday, May 6.

This morning dawned clear and bright; all nature seemed refreshed by yesterday's rain, and we started joyfully on our journey once more. We came through Iconium early in the day, are camping in Lucas County, near a beautiful farmhouse. We expect to stay here until Monday, as we do not intend to travel on Sundays.

It is a beautiful moonlight night, some one proposes a walk. As Cash is giving Winthrop his first lessons in flirtation, they, of course, go together; Sim and Neelie, Miss Milburn and Ezra are the next to start, and Frank is waiting to go with me. Hill stays in camp, in conversation with Mr. Kerfoot and Mr. Milburn.

He is more like an old man than the boy that he is, not twenty yet. After we had gone a short distance,

110

Miss Milburn asked to be excused, and returned to camp; Ezra, of course, going with her.

We walked on for a mile or more, enjoying the beautiful moonlight, and having lots of fun, as happy young people will have. When we returned and I had said good-night to the others, I climbed into the wagon to finish my writing for the day by the light of the lantern.

The front of Mr. Milburn's wagon almost touches the back of ours, forming an angle. I had been writing a few moments when I heard sobbing. I was out in a jiffy, and had gone to the front of their wagon without stopping to think whether I was intruding. "May I come in?" I asked, as I stepped upon the wagon-tongue.

"Oh, yes, come in, Miss Sallie, but I am ashamed to let you see me crying, somehow I could not help it. I felt so lonely and homesick."

"I am sorry you feel lonely and homesick. Did any of us say, or do anything this evening that could have hurt you?"

"Oh, no; not at all, only I always feel that I am one too many, when I am with you all; you seem so light-hearted and happy, so free from care, so full of life and fun, that I feel that I am a damper to your joyousness, for I cannot get over feeling homesick and sad, especially when night comes."

"How sweetly Ernest sleeps, and how much he seems to enjoy this manner of life."

"Yes; he is a great comfort to me, as well as a great care. He is dearer to me than to any one else in the world; his father seems to be weaned from him, since they have been separated so long. He has not seen him more than half a dozen times since his mother died. I feel that he is altogether mine. May God help me to train him for Heaven. He will never know what I have sacrificed for him. I have a mind to tell you, if you care to hear, why I am here, and why I am not happy."

"It may perhaps relieve you, and lighten the burden, to share it."

And then she told me what I will record to-morrow, for it is almost midnight, and mother has been asleep for two hours, and I must hie me to bed.

MISS MILBURN'S LOVE STORY.

"Of course you have heard about my engagement to Jim Miller. I know it has been talked about."

"Yes; I have heard the matter discussed."

"We have been engaged two years, and were to be married next month. He insisted that I must give up Ernest to mother. I felt that I would be violating a sacred trust, and that mother is too old to have the care of such a child, and I told him so. We quarreled, and while I was feeling hurt and indignant, I told Brother John I would go with him to Montana. He gladly accepted my offer, and his wife was so glad John would have some one to take care of him if he got sick. So here I am and I know I ought not to have come, for Jim Miller is dearer to me than my own life."

"I am so sorry for you, yet I believe that in some way it will be for the best, you know the promise, 'All things work together for good, to those who love the Lord."

"I will try to believe it. You have done me good, Miss Sallie. I am glad you came. Come again."

*   *   *   *   *

Sunday, May 7.

"Remember the Sabbath Day to keep it holy." Have we obeyed this command to-day? I fear not. We are all, or very nearly all, professing Christians, yet we have had no public worship in our camp to-day, but we have all, to some extent, desecrated the day by work.

Deeds of mercy and necessity may be done on the Sabbath Day without sin, and mother says, "It is very necessary that our soiled clothes, sheets and pillow-cases should be washed, and that cleanliness is next to godliness."

The question comes to me, Why is it that Christians are so loath to talk of the things that pertain to their spiritual life, and eternal welfare? Why so backward about introducing a service of worship, when so well aware it would meet with the approval of all?

I felt that Mr. Kerfoot was the one to suggest a service of prayer and praise, and reading the Scriptures. Perhaps he thought some of the ladies would mention it, so all were silent, and it is numbered with the lost opportunities for doing something for our Lord and Master. May he pardon our sins of omission, and may we be permitted to atone for the manner in which we spent our first Sabbath on this trip.

113

We have not traveled, so our teams have rested and done no labor, if we have violated the commandment ourselves.

The weather is perfect; this is another beautiful moonlight night. The young ladies and gentlemen have gone for another walk in the same order as last night, except Frank went with Miss Milburn, and Ezra is waiting for me.

A LETTER TO BROTHER MAC.

Monday, May 8.

I left camp very early, and walked on alone, that I may write to Brother Mac before the wagons overtake me. I am seated in a comfortable fence corner, and here goes for my letter:

LUCAS COUNTY, IOWA, May 8, 1865.

DEAR BROTHER: We were delayed several days after the time set for starting, when we wrote you to meet us at Council Bluffs by the 10th. We thought I would better write, that you may know we are on the way, and hope to meet you by the 15th or the 16th. You must possess your soul with patience, if you get there before we do, and have to wait. I could write a long letter, I have so much to tell you, but will wait until we meet. Mother seems in better health and spirits than she has since you went into the army. We are enjoying the trip very much, and I find myself feeling sorry for the people that have to stay at home, and cannot travel and camp out. Good-bye until next week. With sincerest love,

Your sister,
SARAH.

The wagons are coming in sight, just as my letter is finished and addressed, and ready to mail at the next post-office. My pony is in harness to-day, as one of the work horses is a little lame, so I will have to ride in the wagon or walk. As the morning is so fine I will walk until I begin to tire.

Evening.

Cash joined me in my walk, and we walked until noon. How wisely planned are these physical bodies of ours, how easily inured to the burdens they must bear. Before we started on this trip, such a walk as we took this morning would have completely prostrated us; now, we did not feel any inconvenience from the unusual exercise.

Frank invited us, Cash and I, to ride in his wagon this afternoon. We accepted the invitation, and made an emigrant visit. He had arranged his wagon for our convenience and comfort, and we spent a very pleasant afternoon. Frank mailed my letter at Charaton, and on his way back bought candy and nuts for a treat for his visitors, which we, of course, enjoyed exceedingly.

I should not care to ride in an ox-wagon all the way across the plains, but for half a day, once in a while, it is a pleasant change, especially when so delightfully entertained. The afternoon passed quickly. We are camping near a large party of emigrants, some of the men came to our camp. They look tough; they are from Pike County, Missouri, on their way to Oregon.

*   *   *   *   *

115

Tuesday, May 9.

A beautiful day for horseback riding, until late this afternoon, when it commenced blowing a perfect gale, too severe to travel, so we drove into camp early. We came through Ottawa and Osceola, are camping in Clark County.

*   *   *   *   *

Wednesday, May 10.

A very cold day for this time of year, too cold to think of riding horseback, so we all took passage in the wagons. As we have plenty to read, and lots of visiting to do, it is no hardship to ride in the wagon for a day.

The boys have made a splendid camp-fire, and we are getting thawed out, cheered, and ready for a jolly evening. There was just one stunted oak left standing, away out here in this great expanse of prairie—for our especial benefit, it seems. The boys cut it down, and taking the trunk for a back-log, the top and branches to build the fire, we have a glorious camp-fire away out here in Union County, Iowa. It is surprising to find Iowa so sparsely settled, we travel sometimes half a day and do not see a home. There are always a few farms near the towns. The settlements are the only breaks in the monotonous landscape.

Oh, the tedious, tiresome monotony of these vast extended prairies: To look out and away, over these seemingly endless levels, as far as the eye can reach, and see only grass, grass everywhere, with beautiful prairie flowers, of course, but the flowers cannot be seen in the distance. No earthly consideration would induce me to make a home on any of these immense prairie levels. How my eyes long for a sight of beautiful trees, and running streams of water; how delightful to stroll in the woods once more.

*   *   *   *   *

Thursday, May 11.

The wish expressed last evening is realized in a manner. We are camping in a strip of timber along the banks of a creek—or branch, rather. But then it is such a slow-going stream, not at all limpid, clear, or sparkling as a brook ought to be. It can hardly be called a running stream, for it goes too slowly. I think creeping or crawling would be more appropriate. We came through Afton to-day.

THE ICARIAN COMMUNITY.

Friday, May 12.

Brother Hillhouse's birthday. He is twenty years old. We made a birthday cake for him last night. We divided it into twenty pieces at lunch to-day, and there was just enough to go around and leave two pieces for himself. The girls say we must have some kind of a jollification to-night. I hope they will leave me out, for I want to write about the "Icarian Community." We came through Queen City this morning, and this afternoon came to a town of French people, called "The Icarian Community."

(Call to dinner.)

Later: They have excused me.

117

But why Icarian? I cannot understand, for certainly they did not impress me as high flyers, neither as flyers at all. They seemed the most humdrum, slow-going, even-tenor, all-dressed-alike folks I have ever seen. Every dwelling is exactly alike, log-cabins of one room, with one door, one window, a fire-place with stick chimney. I rode close by the open doors of some of the houses, and tried to talk with the women, but we could not understand each other at all. The floors, windows and everything in the houses were scrupulously clean, but not one bit of brightness or color, not a thread of carpet, or a rug, and all the women's and girls' dresses made of heavy blue denim, with white kerchiefs around the shoulders and pinned across the front of the waist, the skirt above the ankles, and very narrow and heavy thick-soled shoes. The men and boys all looked alike too, but I did not observe them closely enough to describe them.

There are several large, long buildings, one with a large bell in belfry on top of building. They are dining-hall, town-hall, school-house and two others. I did not learn what they are used for. All the buildings are one story, of the plainest architecture, for the one purpose of shelter from sun and storm. There is not a thing to ornament or beautify, not a shade-tree or flower, yet everything—men, women, children, houses, yards and streets—are as clean as they can be made.

They are peaceable, law-abiding citizens, live entirely independent of the people of adjoining neighborhoods. They are supposed to be wealthy; the town is the center of well-cultivated and well-stocked farms.

The principle upon which the community is founded is "Brotherly Love", a sort of co-operative communism, in which all things are the common property of all. They live upon what their farms produce, have vast herds of cattle and sheep, a fine site for their town, and seem the picture of contentment, which is better than riches.

We stopped within sight of Quincy, and another camping outfit. We soon learned they are Mr. Harding and Mr. Morrison and family, from Lewis County. We are acquainted with Mr. Harding and have often heard of the Morrisons.

Mr. Morrison and Mr. Harding came over, and the men have had a sociable, gossiping time this evening; the men can surpass the women gossiping any time, notwithstanding the general belief to the contrary. The young folks have been playing games to celebrate Hillhouse's birthday. They had hard work to get him to join them.

A SWING AMONG THE TREES.

Saturday, May 13.

We drove only until noon, and stopped to stay over Sunday, so that we can do our washing and baking, without violating the Sabbath. We do not have collars and cuffs, and fine starched things to do up, but we have a great many pocket handkerchiefs, aprons, stockings, etc. We have pretty bead collars made of black and white beads, tied with a ribbon, that always look nice and do not get soiled. We are in a beautiful grove of trees. The boys have put up a swing. There is nothing in the way of play that I enjoy as I do a good high swing. There are plenty of boys to swing us as high as we want to go. I fear the Sabbath will be desecrated with play to-morrow, if not with work, for the temptation to swing will be hard to resist.

*   *   *   *   *

Sunday, May 14.

The horses went off two or three miles last night, the men were all off bright and early this morning hunting them. Mr. Kerfoot found them, and came back about nine o'clock. By the time they were all here the morning's work was finished and we were ready—for what?

A day to spend in rest and service for the Master? Oh, no. A day spent in swinging, frivolous conversation, and fun. I am ashamed to tell it, but it is nevertheless true, and I believe we all thought less about a service of worship than we did last Sunday. It is so hard to get right, if we do not start right.

We have visitors in camp to-night, two gentlemen from Clark County, neighbors of the Kerfoots—Mr. Suitor and Mr. Rain. They started for the gold mines in Montana two or three weeks ago. After reaching the Missouri River they heard such frightful stories of Indian depredations being committed on the plains that they sold their outfit for what they could get, and are returning home on horseback. Poor fellows, how I pity any man that has so little grit. I should think they would be ashamed to show their faces to their neighbors, and say, "We were afraid, so we came back home."

I believe Mrs. Kerfoot is the only one of our party who would be willing to turn back, and perhaps she would not if it were put to the test. We would not like to be scalped and butchered by the Indians, but it does seem so cowardly to run away from a possible danger. "The everlasting arms are underneath." God can, and will, take care of us as well on the plains as anywhere. He is leading us through unknown paths. We can trust Him. Heaven is as near one place as another.

Our second Sunday has not been much of an improvement on our first. The first we worked, to-day we have played. The boys swung us all morning, until we were ready to "holler nuff." We had Sunday dinner between two and three o'clock, then we wrote letters to friends at home, read until sleepy, took a nap of an hour, then Mr. Suitor and Mr. Rain came, and we listened to their frightful stories of what the Indians are doing to emigrants.

I left them in disgust, to come and record our misdoings of this, our second, Sunday on the road. It is almost bedtime, and I must make the beds, for we are early to bed and early to rise while on this trip.

A FATAL ACCIDENT.

Monday, May 15.

Alas, alas! How can I write the disastrous happenings of this day? My hand trembles and my pencil refuses to write intelligibly when I attempt to record the sad, oh, so sad, accident that has befallen us. We parted from our visitors this morning, and started on our way, feeling rested and glad to be journeying on again. How little we knew of what a day would bring forth. We stopped for lunch at noon in a little vale, or depression, on the prairie, but where there was no water. Just as we had finished our lunch, Neelie came, she said, to see if we could make an exchange for the afternoon, her mother riding with mine, and I with the young folks in the family wagon. Of course it was soon arranged, and I told her I would come as soon as I helped mother put things away. (We sometimes visit in this way.) Mrs. Kerfoot soon came around, and when everything was ready I started to go to their wagon. It was the last one in the train. As I was passing Mr. Milburn's wagon he called to me to "Come and get a drink of water." He had taken a long walk, and found clear, pure water, not very cold, but much better than none at all. I gratefully accepted a cup. He and his sister then invited me to ride with them. I told them of my engagement with Neelie, and, of course, they excused me. Oh, that I had accepted their invitation; just such a little thing as that might have prevented this dreadful accident. Such great events turn on such little hinges sometimes. About three o'clock in the afternoon, as we were plodding along after the fashion of emigrant teams, we young people in the last wagon, having a jolly sociable time, with song and laughter, fun and merriment, the front wagons stopped. Ezra, who was driving, turned out of the road and passed some of the wagons to see what the trouble was. Mr. Kerfoot came running toward us, calling to Neelie, "Get the camphor, daughter, Mr. Milburn has shot himself somehow, and has fainted."

Ezra got out to go with him and Neelie asked, "Shall we come, too, papa?"

"No, my daughter, you girls would better stay here, your ma and Mrs. Raymond are with Gus, and they will know what to do."

Before he had finished what he was saying they were running to the place of the accident. We could only wait, hoping and praying, oh, so earnestly, that it might not prove so serious as Mr. Kerfoot's manner and tone caused us to fear. Afterward, Winthrop came to us; he was pale, with compressed lips, and sad eyes; he came up close, leaned upon the wagon wheel, and said in a low tone, "He is dead." Oh, how dreadful. We all left the wagon and went to the front as fast as we could.

I have gathered from witnesses the following account of how it happened. There was a flock of prairie chickens ahead of the wagons to the left of the road. Mr. Milburn and several of the boys took their guns and were going to try to thin their number. The wagons had not halted, but were moving slowly on, the hunters had gone on a little in advance of the wagons, they tried to fire all together, one of the boys snapped two caps on his gun, it failed to go off, so he threw the gun into the front wagon, and took his whip, in disgust. The wagon had moved on to where Mr. Milburn was standing with his gun raised; there was a shot, Mr. Milburn dropped to his knees, turned and looked at his sister, saying, "Gus, I am shot." And fell forward on his face. She was in the next wagon.

BEREAVEMENT.

Gus screamed, jumped from the wagon, ran to her brother, and raised his head in her arms. All who were near enough to hear her scream ran to them and she said, "John has hurt himself with his gun and has fainted, bring restoratives quick."

In a few seconds, there were half a dozen bottles, with brandy, camphor, ammonia there, and every effort was made to restore him, but all in vain. He died instantly and without a struggle.

When Mr. Kerfoot knew he was dead, he looked for the wound and found a bullet-hole between his shoulders. Just then one of the boys picked up his gun where he had dropped it and exclaimed, "It was not this gun that did the mischief, for it is cold, and the load is in it."

On looking around to find where the deadly shot had come from, some one took hold of the gun in the front wagon. "Why, this gun is warm. It must have been this gun went off."

"Oh, no; it could not have been that gun, for there was no cap on it," said the boy who had thrown the gun there.

Circumstances proved that it was the gun without a cap that did the fatal shooting. I would have supposed, as the boy did, that it was perfectly harmless without a cap. I have heard it said, "It is the unloaded gun, or the one that is supposed to be unloaded, that generally does the mischief." No doubt the hammer was thrown back when he threw it in the wagon. On investigating we found a rut in the wheel-track just where he fell. It is possible that when the front wheel dropped into the rut with a jolt the hammer fell, igniting the powder, either by the combustible matter that stuck, or by the flash occasioned by the metal striking together. Mr. Milburn was not opposite the wagon when he raised his gun to shoot, but the wagons were moving slowly and the front one came up with him as he was taking aim, and that was why Gus thought it was his own gun. She saw the smoke rise, he stumbled and fell to his knees, she called to him. "Why, John, what made you fall?"

He looked around at her and said, "Oh, Gus, I am shot." The last words he spoke.

How hard to be reconciled to such a dispensation when such a little thing could have prevented it, only one step in either direction, or the gun pointed the other way. Why, oh, why, has this awful thing happened?

The poor boy seems to be as heart-stricken as Gus. In her unselfish grief she has been trying to comfort him.

I have read of a minister of the Gospel "who dreamed that he died; after entering the gates of Heaven he was led into a large empty room, on the walls of which his whole life was spread out as a panorama. He saw all the events of his life, and many that had been hard to understand in his lifetime were here made clear, and through it all the guiding, protecting hand of God had been over him." Perhaps Mr. Milburn is saved from a worse fate.

We were about three miles from Frankfort when the accident happened. We came on here as soon as possible—a sorrowing, and oh, so sorrowful, procession now. It does not seem that we can ever be the merry party that we have been. Winthrop had been riding Dick; he stood there, ready, saddled and bridled when Mr. Milburn fell; Frank mounted my pony and rode as fast as he could go to Frankfort to get a doctor. Mr. Milburn was dead before he was out of sight. We met them as we came. A room has been rented and Mr. Milburn prepared for his last long sleep. The people of Frankfort are very kind, and sympathetic.

A FUNERAL.

Tuesday, May 16.

The boys sat up with the corpse last night. I stayed with Gus. We had only just shut ourselves in when a terrific storm came upon us; the wind blew, and the rain fell in torrents. Before eleven o'clock it had passed; soon after Gus slept heavily. It seemed hours before I slept. Very early this morning Gus awakened me praying. How surely do the sorrows of this life drive us to the mercy-seat for comfort, refuge and strength.

"Had earth no thorns among its flowers,
And life no fount of tears,
We might forget our better home
Beyond this vale of tears."

What a precious, what a comforting, satisfying faith the Presbyterian faith must be, if one can really and conscientiously accept it. According to their belief one never dies, nothing ever happens without God's providence, approval, and foreknowledge that it will happen in just that way.

I wish I could accept such a faith, and believe it, but I cannot. I do not believe it was ordained that Mr. Milburn should die in that way and at that time. I believe it was an accident that might have been prevented by the most trivial circumstance. The laws of nature are inexorable. If a bullet is shot into a vital part of the body it kills. Yet God is able to bring good out of this seemingly great and grievous evil. I do not know which suffers most—the poor boy whose gun did the deed or Gus. They seem to take comfort in each other's society, and are together the most of the time to-day. I am so sorry for both of them.

The funeral services of the Presbyterian Church were held at two o'clock this afternoon, a resident minister officiating. Mr. Milburn was very nicely laid away, and his grave marked and enclosed with a neat, strong fence before Gus and I left the cemetery. The people have been so very kind. The funeral was largely attended for a stranger in a strange place. There is no telegraph office here, so we have had to write letters instead of sending telegrams.

I believe Gus's plans are to go on with us to the Missouri River, sell her outfit, and return home by steamboat down the Missouri River, up the Mississippi to Canton, where friends will meet her and go with her to Etna.

*   *   *   *   *

Wednesday, May 17.

Another night with Gus. She wakes in the morning to weep. We started once more on our now sad journey. I have ridden with Gus all day. We do not hear the sound of song and laughter as we did last week; we all seem to be under a pall. We came through Redoak this morning, are camping in a beautiful place, near a pleasant, homelike farmhouse. The weather is perfect.

*   *   *   *   *

The friends that stayed with us Sunday night told us that the authorities are not allowing emigrants to take the northern route, because of the Indian depredations that have been committed on that route. That if we went to Council Bluffs we would have to come down the river to Platsmouth to get on the southern route. So we changed our course accordingly.

We came through Whitecloud, Glenwood and Pacific City to-day. At Whitecloud I made a few purchases, traded with a little German merchant who crossed the plains a year ago; he says we have a delightful trip before us. He expects to go again to the Rocky Mountains, and make his home there, as soon as he can sell out and settle up his business here.

Just before we came to Glenwood, as the girls passed on their ponies, Gus said to me, "Sallie, go ride your pony, too; you have not had a ride for several days. Pardon me if I have been selfish in my great sorrow."

"No, Gus, I would rather stay with you than to ride Dick, as long as you need me."

"Thank you, dear; your company has been very grateful to me, but now I would really enjoy seeing you ride through Glenwood."

To please her, and myself, too, I soon had saddled and mounted Dick and overtaken the girls. As we were riding through Glenwood a photographer sent a messenger to request us to "Please stop five minutes and let him take our picture." We rode to the position indicated, doffed our sun-bonnets, and looked as

128

pleasant as we could. We did not wait to see the proof, and I expect he was disappointed.

Pacific City is on the Missouri bottom, or lowlands. Above the town are the highest bluffs I have ever seen. We hitched our ponies and climbed to the top. The view was magnificently grand, the sun sinking in the west, the river could be seen in the distance, with large trees on the banks, the lowland between the bluffs and the trees was dotted with cattle and horses grazing, here and there a pond or small lake with its waters shining and sparkling in the glimmering sunset, the city below us in the shadow of the bluffs. Everything was so sweet and peaceful, we were more than paid for our climb. The wagons had passed before we came down, so we mounted and hastened to overtake them before driving into camp.

ON THE BANKS OF THE BIG MUDDY.

Our journey across Iowa at an end, we are on the banks of the Big Muddy, opposite Platsmouth. We will stay here until Gus's things are sold, and we have seen her off on the steamboat. I stay with her nights, and this afternoon is the first time I have left her since the 15th.

*   *   *   *   *

Friday, May 19.

I went over to Platsmouth on the ferryboat this morning with some friends that are camping near us, to do some shopping for Gus. I bought a black bonnet, crèpe veil and collar, and material for black suit, which we will make up in camp, as there is a dress-maker with us. I was away about five hours and came back tired and hungry. The weather is perfect. We have a very pleasant place to camp, and pleasant people camping near us. We are surrounded on all sides by emigrants' camps, and still they come. It seems like a young town, only the houses are built of canvas instead of lumber, brick or stone. The boys have put up a swing, but I have no time for swinging to-day.

*   *   *   *   *

Saturday, May 20.

We have had a very, very busy day. Mr. Kerfoot has sold Gus's wagon and team (three yoke of oxen) for $550, a good price every one says. More than they cost them, I believe. The freight will be sold at auction. We have all helped with Gus's suit and it is almost finished. Hillhouse went up to Council Bluffs this morning, expecting to bring Brother Mac back with him. Instead of finding him he got a letter—also the one I wrote a week ago—saying he was not coming. He has decided to study medicine and will come west when he is an M.D. We are disappointed, of course, yet perhaps it is for the best—we must try and believe so anyway. Most perfect weather.

The Morrison and Harding outfit have come, also several other families from Lewis and Clark counties. The Kerfoots are acquainted with some of them. They had heard of the sad accident. Some of them were friends of Mr. Milburn.

OUR LAST DAY WITH MISS MILBURN.

Sunday, May 21.

Mr. Thatcher and his wife came to call upon Gus this afternoon, and invited her to their home in Platsmouth to stay until she takes the steamboat for home. Mr. Thatcher and Mr. Milburn have been friends for years. She accepted their invitation and will go there to-morrow.

As the people from different camps were sitting around an immense camp-fire, not far from our wagons, someone proposed music. Some of the men in Mr. Clark's camp are fine musicians, they brought their violin and flute, and gave several instrumental pieces, then some familiar songs were sung and someone started "Just Before the Battle, Mother." They had sung two verses when I heard a shriek from Gus's wagon. I hastened to see what was the matter. "Oh, Sallie, tell them to please not sing that, I cannot bear it. Dear Brother John used to sing it so much. It breaks my heart to hear it now."

I sent Winthrop, who had followed me, to ask them to stop singing. Poor Gus, she was more overcome than I have seen her since her bereavement.

*　　　*　　　*　　　*　　　*

Monday, May 22.

Mr. Kerfoot, Cash, Neelie, Ezra and I came with Gus to Platsmouth. She said good-bye to mother, Mrs. Kerfoot and the others this morning. All were sorry to part with her. She has become very dear to us all. Gus's freight was brought over in the wagon and sold at public auction and brought good figures, thanks to Mr. Thatcher, who, when he saw anything going below its real value, bid it in himself. He has a grocery store. He and Mr. Kerfoot have attended to all business transactions for Gus, so that she has not been bothered at all, and have done better for her than they could have done for themselves.

We have had a quiet, pleasant day with Gus at Mrs. Thatcher's home. She is very kind, and has invited us girls to stay with Gus until she takes the boat for home, and Gus begged us to stay with her as long as possible; so Cash and I are staying all night, and will see her on board the boat to-morrow morning. Neelie has returned to camp with her father and Ezra.

Ernest is a great care and worries his auntie. He will not stay in the house, and she cannot bear to have him out of her sight for fear something will happen to him; she has just now undressed him, heard his little prayer, and put him to bed in the next room. So I hope we can have uninterrupted quiet for awhile.

*   *   *   *   *

Tuesday, May 23.

Mr. and Mrs. Thatcher, Cash and I came with Gus and Ernest to the steamboat. We parted with them about nine o'clock on board the "Sioux City." Dear friend, I have become greatly attached to her, in the three weeks we have been so intimately associated. May God grant her a quick and safe journey home. We cannot hope it will be a happy one.

NOTE.—Miss Milburn and her lover were married about six months after her return, and have lived happily, etc.

132

Cash and I came directly to camp, after saying good-bye to Gus; found every one busy getting ready for an early start to-morrow. We have been here almost a week, yet I have not had time to try the fine swing the boys put up the next day after we came here until this afternoon. The camps that were here over Sunday are all gone except those that will travel with us. It is probable there will be half a dozen more camps here before night. It is surprising to see what a great number of people are going west this Spring.

We hope to start very early to-morrow morning. I trust our party will not be so much like a funeral procession as it has been since the 15th. Vain regrets cannot remedy the past, and I believe it is our duty to be as cheerful and happy as possible in this life.

WE HAVE OUR PICTURES TAKEN.

Wednesday, May 24.

We were up with the earliest dawn, and our own individual outfit ready for a very early start, yet it was the middle of the forenoon before all the wagons were landed on the west bank of the Missouri. It takes a long while to ferry fifteen wagons across the river. We girls rode our ponies onto the ferryboat. They behaved as if they had been used to ferryboats all their lives. As we were waiting near the landing a stranger[1] came, apologized for speaking to us, and asked, "Are you going to Montana?"

---

[1] This man is mentioned here because of what happened to him before he reached his journey's end.

133

"No, sir, our destination is California, or Oregon; we are not fully decided which."

"Oh, you ought to go to Montana; that is the place to get rich."

He told of his marvelous success in that country since 1863; the Indians were mentioned. He spoke of them with such contempt; said he would rather kill an Indian than a good dog. Says he left a wife and six children in Iowa, the oldest boy about fourteen who wanted very much to go with his father, but his mother needed him. Last night he came into his father's camp. He had run away from home; says he is going to Montana, too. His father told it as if he thought it smart, and a good joke. What sorrow and anxiety his poor mother is no doubt suffering.

Cash, Neelie, Sim Buford, Ezra, Frank, Winthrop and I while waiting in Platsmouth went to a photographer's and had our pictures taken; tintype, of course, all in one group, then each one alone, then Sim and Neelie together and Cash and I on our ponies. We only came five miles after our rush to get an early start. There are nine families and fifteen wagons in our train now. Miss Mary Gatewood has a pony for her especial use, so there will be four of us to ride horseback. There are enough wagons now to make quite a respectable corral. I did suppose, as we had been resting so long, we would make a long drive. Feed for the stock is very good here, and as it is fifteen miles to the next good camping place, where there is plenty of water and feed, it has been decided that we stay here until to-morrow. The boys have put up the inevitable swing, and we have concluded "that what cannot be cured must be endured." So we will make the best of it, but certainly at this rate we will not reach our destination before it is cold weather.

* * * * *

Thursday, May 25.

Oh, dear; here we are yet, only five miles from Platsmouth. Morrison and Harding have lost two fine cows, half a dozen men have been hunting them all day, but without success. There is not a doubt but that they have been stolen. Our stock will have to be herded, hereafter, to guard against thieves. We have spent the day reading, writing, sleeping, swinging, and getting acquainted with our neighbors. The Morrison family wagon is just in front of us, and the Kerfoot's just behind, so we are to have the most pleasant neighbors possible to camp next to us. Mrs. Morrison is almost as pretty as Cash, although the mother of four children; she is so bright and cheerful, so full of life and fun, she will be great on a trip like this. Mr. Morrison has an impediment in his speech, and when he is excited—like he is this evening, because they cannot find their cows—he stutters dreadfully, and will say, "Or sir, or sir, or sir," until it is hard to keep from laughing. In ordinary conversation and when not excited, he talks as straight as any one. He seems so fond and proud of his wife and children I like him. Neelie and Sim, and Frank and I took a stroll this afternoon in search of wild flowers. They are few and far between, yet we enjoyed the walk through the woods in this lovely springtime weather.

A YANKEE HOMESTEAD.

Friday, May 26.

We came fifteen miles, are camping on a high rolling prairie, not a tree or shrub within sight; we are near a neat white farmhouse. Everything seems to be very new, but does not have that "lick and a promise" appearance that so many farmhouses in Nebraska have. Things seem to be shipshape, the house completed and nicely painted, a new picket-fence, and everything on the place—barns, hen-house, etc., all seem well built, as if the owners are expecting to make a permanent home. I would prefer a home not quite so isolated and far away from anywhere. There do not seem to be any women about the place, perhaps they are coming when everything is ready for their comfort.

*   *   *   *   *

Saturday, May 27.

We came to Ashland, on Salt River, only a fifteen-mile drive, got here soon after noon and will stay over Sunday. Several of us young folks went fishing this afternoon. I have often gone fishing but do not remember ever catching anything of any consequence, or having any luck, as the boys say, so imagine my excitement and surprise when the fish began to bite, and I drew them out almost as fast as I could get my hook baited. Frank baited my hook and strung the fish on a forked willow switch. After I had caught six or eight they seem so dry and miserable I thought they would feel better in the water, so stuck the willow in the bank, so that the fish were in shallow water. I caught another fish and went to put it with the others, when lo, they were all gone. I could have cried, and the rest all laughed—well, I shall try again.

After securing the one I had—and leaving it on dry ground, I threw in my hook, and almost immediately I had caught something so large and heavy I could not draw it out and had to call for assistance. I was fearful it was a mud-turtle or something else than a fish, but it proved to be a fine, large fish, larger than all the small fish I had lost put together. When Frank had taken it from the hook, and strung it with the little one, I said, "Now I am going, before this fish gets away." All had fairly good catches, but none that compared with my big fish. There are about twenty corrals within sight, each of from twelve to twenty wagons. Ashland is a miserable looking place, the houses log-cabins with dirt roofs. One store, where dry-goods, groceries, and whiskey are sold, and a blacksmith shop are all the business houses. I do not see anything that would pass muster as a hotel.

*　　　*　　　*　　　*　　　*

Sunday, May 28.

All the trains that camped near us last night, except one, have gone on their way, Sunday though it is. I am glad there are some people going West who regard the Sabbath day. Some of our young people went fishing, and some went rowing on the river in a canoe or small boat the boys hired. It has been a day of sweet rest, a quiet peaceful Sabbath.

*　　　*　　　*　　　*　　　*

Traveled all day, and made a long drive without meeting anyone or passing a single habitation. We are camping near—what the people west of the Missouri River call—a ranch. There is a long, low log-cabin, with dirt roof, a corral, or inclosure for stock, with very high fence, and two or three wells of water in the vicinity, and that is all. No vegetable garden, no fields of grain, nor anything to make it look like farming. I think it is a stage-station, and the people who occupy do not expect to stay very long.

There are three other camps near, the people of the other trains are having an emigrant ball, or dance, in a room they have hired. They sent a committee with a polite invitation to our camp for us to join them, which was as politely declined. They are strangers, and the conduct of some of the women is not ladylike, to say the least.

WE MEET A FRIEND.

Tuesday, May 30.

We girls were riding in advance of the wagons when we saw a long freight train coming. We stopped to let our ponies graze until they would pass. I glanced at the driver on the second wagon and recognized an acquaintance. "Why, girls, that is Kid Short," I exclaimed.

He looked at me so funny, and began to scramble down from his high perch.

138

"Why, Miss Sallie, I could not believe my eyes at first. Where did you drop from?" shaking hands with each of us.

"Didn't drop from anywhere; have been thirty days getting here by the slow pace of an ox-train. Sim Buford and some more boys that you know are with the train you see coming."

He soon said good-bye to us, spoke to a man on horseback, who dismounted, gave him his horse and climbed to the seat Mr. Short had vacated in the front of the freight wagon, drawn by eight mules, while Kid hurried off to see the boys. He and Sim have been neighbors, schoolmates, and intimate friends all their lives. Sim says Kid is homesick and expects to go home as soon as he can after reaching Omaha. He has been freighting from Omaha to Kearney, and has been away from home since last Fall. We are camping near another station, with the same trains we camped near last night not far off.

*   *   *   *   *

Wednesday, May 31.

We are camping in the valley of the Platte. We are obliged to stop at the stage-stations to get water for ourselves and the stock from the wells. The water is very good, clear and cold. The same trains that have been camping near us since we left Ashland are here again to-night. Two of the women called upon us awhile ago. We were not favorably impressed. They are loud, boisterous and unladylike; they speak to strange gentlemen with all the familiarity of old acquaintances.

According to Thackeray, they are "Becky Sharp" kind of women.

* * * * *

Thursday, June 1.

Our little village on wheels has stopped near a large two-story log-house that was built in the early fifties for a wayside tavern; there are fifteen rooms; there are frightful stories told of dark deeds having been committed under that roof, of unwary travelers homeward bound from California that never reached home, but whether true or not I cannot say. The people of the other trains are having a dance in the large dining-room of the old house.

* * * * *

Friday, June 2.

As Ezra and I were riding in front of the train we came to where a man was sitting on the ground hugging his knees, two men were standing near trying to talk to him, seemingly. As we rode up one of them came toward us, saying, "That is an Indian, over there." We rode close to him, and Ezra said, "How;" but he did not even grunt. He was very disappointing as the "Noble Red Man" we read about. He wore an old ragged federal suit, cap and all. There were no feathers, beads nor blankets. He was not black like a negro, more of a brown, and a different shade from the mulatto. He was ugly as sin.

140

ON THE BANKS OF THE PLATTE.

Here we are on the Platte with about two hundred wagons in sight. We are now on what is known as "The Plains." My idea of the plains has been very erroneous, for I thought they were one continuous level or plain as far as the eye could reach, no hills nor hollows, but it is nothing else than the Platte River Valley with high bluffs on either side. There is some timber on the banks, but the timber of any consequence is on the islands in the middle of the river, out of reach of the axe of the emigrant. This is the junction of the roads from St. Joe and Plattsmouth, and that is why there are so many wagons here to-night. Surely, among all these people there must be a minister of the Gospel, so perhaps we will have public worship to-morrow. Our trip grows more interesting, even Mrs. Kerfoot seems interested, as so many people are going West, it must be the thing to do.

*　　　*　　　*　　　*　　　*

Sunday, June 4.

We are organized into a company of forty-five wagons, a captain and orderly sergeant have been elected, and hereafter we will travel by system. Mr. Hardinbrooke is our captain. He has gone on this trip before; he is taking his wife and little girl with him to Montana. A Mr. Davis is our orderly sergeant.

We are now coming into a country infested with Indians, so it is required by Government officials that all emigrants must organize into companies of from forty to sixty wagons, elect captains and try to camp near each other for mutual protection. The grass for stock is unlimited. About twenty of the wagons in our train are freight wagons, belonging to the Walker Brothers, Joe and Milt. Joe has his wife with him. Milt is a bachelor; their sister, Miss Lyde, and a younger brother, De, are with them. They are going to Montana. We have been introduced to Mr. and Mrs. Hardinbrooke, and to the Walkers and their ladies. They are pleasant, intelligent people, and will add much to the pleasure of our party, no doubt. Frank and I went horseback riding this afternoon to the station to get some good water from the well. I cannot drink the river water.

No public worship to-day, although there were so many of us here.

*   *   *   *   *

Monday, June 5.

We were awakened at an early hour this morning with a bugle call. Three companies were organized yesterday; there were about twenty wagons that were not asked to join either party, so they pulled up stakes and left while Frank and I were away. The strange women were of the party; they must be some miles ahead by this time, and I hope they will stay ahead. When our long train of wagons are stretched out upon the road, we make a formidable looking outfit for the Indians to attack. As far as the eye can reach, before us and behind us, there are wagons, wagons, wagons; some drawn by oxen, some by mules, and some by horses. All fall into the slow, sure gait of the

142

oxen. There are whole freight trains drawn by oxen; there are more ox teams than all others.

After our evening meal, a number of us started for a stroll along the bank of the river. Before we reached the river, we were met by a perfect cloud of mosquitoes that literally drove us back. I never came so near being eaten up. There is a strong breeze blowing toward the river, which keeps them from invading the camps, for which I am thankful, otherwise there would be little rest or sleep for us to-night. They are the first mosquitoes we have seen on the road.

* * * * *

Tuesday, June 6.

It is sweet to be awakened with music, if it is only a bugle. Our bugle certainly makes sweet music. The road is becoming very dry and dusty, which makes riding in the wagon rather disagreeable sometimes. Mother and I take turns driving the horses and riding Dick. Rather the most of the time I ride Dick. One of our boys goes out with the herders at night, so one of them is generally sleepy, and sleeps during the day, while the other drives the ox-team.

THE ORDER OF OUR GOING.

Wednesday, June 7.

There is such a sameness in our surroundings that we seem to be stopping in the same place every night, with the same neighbors in front and back of us, and across the corral. When we organized, Mr. Kerfoot's wagons were driven just in front of ours and Mr.

Morrison's just behind ours, so we have the same next-door neighbors, only they have changed places. We are in the central part of the left-hand side of the corral. The wagons occupied by the Walkers and Hardinbrookes are just opposite in the right-hand side of the corral.

We always stop in just this way, if only for an hour at noon—which we do every day for lunch, and to water the stock.

When we halted to-day, the rain began to pour, the stock scattered in every direction. When it stopped raining, the cattle could not all be found in time to start again this afternoon, so we only made half a day's drive. It has commenced raining again, and promises a rainy night. It is not very pleasant camping when it rains, yet it would be much more unpleasant if it did not rain—to lay the dust, refresh the atmosphere, and make the grass grow.

When the captain finds a place for the corral, he rides out where all can see him, and gives the signal, the first and central wagons leave the road; the first to drive to where the captain stands, the other and all behind it cross over a sufficient distance to form the corral by the wagons stopping, so as to form a gateway, for the stock to pass through, turned so that they will not interfere with each other when hitching. The next wagon drives to position, with the right-hand side of cover almost touching the left-hand or back, outer edge of the wagon in front, with tongues of wagons turned out, so that all can be hitched to at one time. In this way the entire corral is formed, meeting at the back an oblong circle, forming a wall or barrier, the cattle cannot break through. The horses are caught and harnessed outside the corral, but the cattle have to be driven inside to be yoked.

*   *   *   *   *

Thursday, June 8.

It rained all night, seemingly without cessation; the wind did not blow, so there was no harm, but lots of good done. I am glad when the rain comes in the night-time, instead of day-time. Where the beds touched the covers they were quite wet this morning.

*   *   *   *   *

Friday, June 9.

We came through a little town—Valley City. There is a very pretty attractive looking house near the road. Cash and I had come on ahead of wagons. Our inclination to enter that pretty home was irresistible, so we dismounted, took off our habits, hitched our ponies, and knocked at the door. A very pleasant lady opened the door and gave us hearty welcome. We told her frankly why we came. She laughed, and said, "I have had callers before, with the same excuse, but you need not apologize, I am glad my home is attractive to strangers."

The gentleman of the house is postmaster, and has his office in the room across the hall from the parlor. While we were there the coach arrived, and the mail was brought in. He did not know we were there, and called to his wife to "Come see this mail." We went with her, and oh, such a mess. They had emptied the mail-sack on some papers that had been spread upon the floor, and such a lot of dilapidated letters and papers I never saw before. I picked up a photograph of an elderly lady, but we could not find the envelope from which it had escaped.

Perhaps some anxious son, away out in the mines, far from home and friends and mother, will look in vain for mother's pictured face, and be so sadly disappointed. I am so sorry for the boy that will miss getting his mother's photograph. She looks like such a sweet, motherly mother. A great many of the letters were past saving; if the owners had been there they could not have deciphered either the address or the written contents, for they were only a mass of pulp; the postmaster said it was, "Because they send such old leaky mail-bags on this route; those post-office folk seem to think any old thing will do for the West, when we ought to have the very best and strongest, because of the long distances they must be carried." All that could be, were carefully handled and spread out to dry; still, they would reach their destination in a very dilapidated condition.

We have made a long drive, are within four miles of Fort Kearney. There are a great many wagons within sight besides our own long train, whichever way we look we can see wagons. The road from Kansas City comes into this road not far from Valley City, and there are as many, or more, coming that way as the way we came. People leaving war-stricken Missouri, no doubt. I have never seen a fort. I do hope Kearney will come up to my expectations.

FORT KEARNEY.

Saturday, June 10.

I was disappointed in Fort Kearney, as I so often am in things I have formed an idea about. There are very comfortable quarters for the soldiers; they have set out trees, and made it quite a pretty place, away out here in the wilderness, but there is no stockade, or place of defense, with mounted cannon, as I had expected.

Sim and I rode horseback through the fort while the wagons kept the road half a mile north of the fort. Only a few of us came by the way of the fort. A soldier gave us a drink of water from a well by the wayside. He seemed a perfect gentleman, but had such a sad expression. We were told that these soldiers were in the Confederate service, were taken prisoners, confined at Rock Island, and enlisted in the Government service to come out here and fight Indians. They are from Georgia and Alabama.

Two families have joined our train and come into corral on the opposite side, just behind the Walkers: Mr. and Mrs. Kennedy—a newly-married couple—and Mr. and Mrs. Bower, with a daughter fourteen and a son five. We only came one and a half miles west of the fort near Kearney City. I do not understand why we have made such a short drive, for the boys say the feed is not good, it has been eaten off so close.

*   *   *   *   *

Sunday, June 11.

We were obliged to leave camp and travel to-day, the first Sunday we have hitched up since we started. It was a case of necessity, as there was not feed for our large herds of cattle and horses. We made only a short drive, just to get good feed for the stock.

We are camping near a station that must seem like a military post, there are so many soldiers. Several soldiers came to our camp this afternoon; they confirmed what we heard yesterday. They are Confederate soldiers, they were prisoners, and their homes are in far-away Georgia and Alabama, and they are desperately homesick. It is a distressing sickness. I have been so homesick that I could not eat or sleep, and a cure was not effected until I was at home again. Then how nice it did seem to be home, and how good everything tasted. I do hope this cruel, homicidal war will soon be over, and these fine-looking Southern gentlemen will be permitted to go to their homes and loved ones, who, no doubt, are waiting and longing for their return. My heart aches for them.

ELEVEN GRAVES.

Monday, June 12.

We stood by the graves of eleven men that were killed last August by the Indians. There was a sort of bulletin-board about midway and at the foot of the graves stating the circumstances of the frightful tragedy. They were a party of fourteen, twelve men and two women, wives of two of the men. They were camped on Plum Creek, a short distance from where the graves are. They were all at breakfast except one man who had gone to the creek for water, he hid in the brush, or there would have been none to tell the tale of the massacre.

There had been no depredations committed on this road all Summer, and emigrants had become careless and traveled in small parties. They did not suspect that an Indian was near until they were surrounded, and the slaughter had commenced. All the men were killed and scalped, and the women taken prisoners. They took what they wanted of the provisions, burned the wagons and ran off with the horses.

The one man that escaped went with all haste to the nearest station for help. The soldiers pursued the Indians, had a fight with them and rescued the women. One of them had seen her husband killed and scalped and was insane when rescued, and died at the station. The other woman was the wife of the man that escaped. They were from St. Joe, Missouri.

Ezra met with quite an accident to-day; he went to sleep while driving the family wagon—he was on guard last night—the horses brought the wheel against a telegraph pole with a sudden jerk that threw him out of his seat and down at the horses' heels—a sudden awakening—with a badly-bruised ankle.

We are in the worst place for Indians on all this road. The bluffs come within half a mile on our left, and hundreds of savages could hide in the hollows; the underbrush and willows are dense along the river banks. There is an island, about a mile in length, that comes so near this side in many places that a man could leap from bank to bank. The island is a thick wood, a place where any number of the dreaded savages could hide, and shoot down the unwary traveler with the guns and ammunition furnished them by the United States Government.

How I would like to climb to the top of those bluffs, and see what is on the other side, but the captain says, "Stay within sight of camp." And I must obey.

A NARROW ESCAPE.

Tuesday, June 13.

Cash, Neelie and I created quite a sensation this morning. We waited, after the train had started, to mount our ponies as we usually do. Cash and I had mounted, but Neelie led her pony, and we went down to the river to water them, Neelie found some beautiful wild flowers, and she insisted upon gathering them. Of course we waited for her. The train was winding round a bend in the road, and the last wagons would soon be out of sight. We insisted that she must come. "The train will be out of sight in five minutes, and we may be cut off by savages in ambush."

She did not scare worth a cent. She led her pony into a little hollow to mount when we saw two men coming toward us as fast as they could ride. Cash rode at an easy canter to meet them, while I waited for Neelie, who was deliberately arranging her flowers so that she would not crush them.

"Those men are coming after us, perhaps there are Indians around." She took her time, just the same.

When the captain saw that the train would soon be out of our sight, he went to Mr. Morrison, who was on horseback, and said, "Ride quietly back and warn those girls of their danger, there are Indians around. They have been seen by the guard, on the island, and by the herders, in the hollows of the bluffs this morning. They

150

would not be safe one minute after the train is out of sight."

They had kept it quiet, as they did not wish to cause unnecessary alarm, for they knew there was no danger, for the Indians knew they were being watched, and besides we are too many for them. Mr. Morrison started, but not quietly; he snatched off his hat, whipping his horse with it, passed Mr. Kerfoot's wagon as fast as his horse could go. Mr. Kerfoot asked, "What is the matter?" Some one said, "Indians!"

He wound the lines round the brake-handle, leaped from his high seat on the front of the wagon, grabbed the first horse in reach, snatched Mr. Gatewood's boy out of the saddle, jumped on the horse and came tearing toward us, lashing the horse with his long whip—his hat flew off soon after he started, but he did not know it. He passed Mr. Morrison, and meeting Cash, he stopped long enough to bring his whip over her horse's haunches with all his might, and sent her flying toward the train. He next met me—for I started, when I saw them coming, and was perhaps a hundreds yards ahead of Neelie—and stopped and said, "Miss Sallie, do you know that we are in the very worst Indian country there is on this road?"

He did not wait for a reply, but went on to Neelie, who was looking all about to see the Indians. He gave her pony a cut with his whip, as he had Cash's, and we went flying over the ground, Neelie's merry laughter pealing forth. Mr. Kerfoot did not speak to either of us. Mr. Morrison had turned back with Cash, and scolded all the way, she said he stuttered and stuttered, until she had hard work to keep from laughing. The captain had stopped the train, and we were greeted with loud cheering and hurrahs.

There was considerable joking about our being anxious for an adventure, and the young men were profuse in their declarations about what they would have done if we had been captured by the Indians. Every one laughed about our "narrow escape," as they called it, except Mr. Kerfoot; he was pale and trembling. It is a shame that he should have been so unnecessarily frightened by our thoughtlessness, and I believe he thinks it was my fault. I wonder what he would have thought if I had left Neelie to come alone?

*   *   *   *   *

Wednesday, June 14.

One of the men found the skull of a human being to-day while we were stopping at noon. It seems horrible to think of one's bones being scattered about in such manner. There is a storm coming; a storm on the plains is something to be dreaded, especially a wind-storm. Old men who have been freighting across the plains for years, say they have seen wagons upset with three tons of freight in a wind-storm. I am more afraid of a wind-storm than of Indians. The boys say I am not afraid of Indians at all.

*   *   *   *   *

Thursday, June 15.

The storm came with great violence last evening; we saw it coming in time to be prepared for it, so there was no damage done. The rain came down in torrents, and made the roads as hard and smooth as a floor, not any mud. It has been fine for horseback riding, everything seems so fresh and clean and pure, and not too warm. Mr. Milt Walker joined us about an hour before camping time. He seems a very pleasant gentleman.

*   *   *   *   *

Friday, June 16.

We had a storm last night, much more terrific than the night of the 14th, yet there was no harm done, more than to frighten some of the women and children. For my part I enjoyed the coming of the storm exceedingly. I never witnessed a storm-scene so sublimely grand. Oh, for the pen of an artist, that I might picture the majesty and grandeur of the coming of that storm.

BEAUX.

Nellie Bower has a pony, and rides with us sometimes. She is a very mature young lady for her age, and very pleasant company. Neelie and I were riding together this morning, while Cash and Nellie Bower rode a short distance ahead. We had been on the road about half an hour when Dr. Fletcher and Milt Walker rode up, requesting the pleasure of our company, in a very formal manner. Of course we smilingly bowed assent, and the doctor rode with Neelie, and Milt with me. It is the first time there has been any formality in our pairing off while riding. The boys sometimes ride with us, but they come informally, we ride as we please, and stop and climb into the wagon when we please, without saying by your leave.

153

I am sorry any such formality has been commenced, for when I want to lope off, and be by myself, I want to feel free to do so, rather than to be constrained to entertain a beau, as we did this morning. Of course, Dr. Fletcher and Mr. Walker have not gone with us thus informally. I presume we succeeded in entertaining them, for when the train turned out for noon, each gentleman looked at his watch and wondered "If it could be possible it is noon?"

Dr. Fletcher is stepbrother of the Walkers—his mother and their father being married. He is physician for our train; an intelligent, handsome man, below medium in size. I think he must be dyspeptic, for he is always finding fault with everything. He seems to admire Neelie very much. We came through Cottonwood this morning. Stopped at noon where the feed is fine, so it has been decided that we stay here until to-morrow. The sky has the appearance of another storm this evening. We have had a busy afternoon.

*   *   *   *   *

Saturday, June 17.

There was a brisk shower last evening about dark, only lasted about half an hour, there was no wind. About midnight the cattle stampeded, the herders do not know what frightened them, but the first thing thought of was Indians, yet there were none visible. Some of the cattle were not found until this afternoon, so here we will have to stay another night.

The bluffs near here are quite high and abrupt. I climbed to the top this morning. I seemed to be away up yonder, when looking down at our corral the people looked like midgets. The bluffs are 150 feet high. I received a beautiful bouquet of wild flowers this evening, but do not know who sent it. The boy said, "A gentleman sent it." But he either could not, or would not, tell what gentleman. Perhaps the one that sent it thought I would know instinctively, but I am certainly in the dark.

Two gentlemen took lunch at our table this afternoon; they are father and son. Hillhouse met them out on the road; they asked him, "Do you know where we can get something to eat? We have had nothing since a very early breakfast."

He brought them to our wagons, and we soon had a lunch ready for them. Their name is Reade, the father's hair and whiskers are as white as snow, otherwise he is not an aged-looking man. They asked questions, and when they found we had not fully decided upon our destination, they insisted that Montana is the place for us. They have been there and are going again with freight. They belong with the Irvine train. Each train goes by the name of its captain, ours is known as "The Hardinbrooke train." Then there is the McMahan train, and the Dickerson train, that always camp within sight of us, for mutual protection. We have not met any of the people from the other trains. The Irvine train—which is very large—are some miles ahead of us. The Reades were hunting cattle, had been as far back as Cottonwood, but without success. The son had a long talk with the boys before leaving camp. After he had gone, Hillhouse came around and took a seat on the wagon-tongue, near where I was engaged in the interesting occupation of the week's mending. I said, "Mr. Read thinks Montana the place for us."

WE DECIDE TO GO TO MONTANA.

"Yes, so do the Walkers, and Mr. Hardinbrooke, and Mr. Morrison, and everyone else that are going to Montana."

"Well, why not go there?"

"I do not like for you and mother to go there, for it will be rough living I expect, but I intend to go as soon as you are settled somewhere near Mr. Kerfoot's folks."

"Just listen to the boy. Mother come here for five minutes, do. What do you think this boy is saying? That he is going to Montana when we are settled in California, or some other place."

"Well, if he is going to Montana, we are going, too. How many women are on their way there in these trains? I reckon it will not be any worse for us than it will be for them."

"All right, if you are both willing to go to Montana, we will change our plans accordingly. It is not as far as California."

And I know he is glad. So it was settled then and there that Montana will be our destination.

*   *   *   *   *

Sunday, June 18.

We started very early this morning, as soon as light, about four o'clock. I think the most of the women were yet in bed. It was a glorious morning, and I did so enjoy my early ride on Dick. We had not been on the road very long when Frank joined me. I told him, "We had decided to go to Montana."

He was silent a moment, then said, "It is the place to go. I do hope we can persuade Uncle Ezra to go there, too."

"I hope he will decide to go with us, for it would be hard to part with all of you now. It would seem almost like leaving home again."

We halted at nine o'clock, had breakfast at ten, started again at twelve. Stopped again at four, and are camping on Fremont's Slough.

*   *   *   *   *

Monday, June 19.

We passed two graves this morning that have been made within a month. The first a man who shot himself accidentally three weeks ago. The other a woman, forty years old, who died one month ago to-day. As I stood beside the lonely graves, I thought of the tears that had been shed, the prayers that had been uttered, the desolation of heart that had been endured by those who had been obliged to go on and leave their loved ones here in this wilderness. How my heart ached for them. My heart went out in thanksgiving and praise to our Heavenly Father that there has been no serious sickness in all these trains with so many people. It is marvelous.

We are camped on the banks of the South Platte. The men have driven the stock across to an island. I do not know if it is because they are afraid of the Indians stampeding them, or that the grass is better. If there should be danger, I presume they would not tell us.

There is a town of prairie dogs near; several of us went to make them a visit, but the boys had been there with their guns shooting at the little things, and frightened them so they would not come out, although we waited in silence until almost dark. I shall make another effort to see them very early in the morning before the boys are awake. I have heard they are early risers, that they come out to greet the rising sun. We met an acquaintance to-day—Will Musgrove—he is on his way to Central City, Colorado. He is night herder for a freight train. The most casual acquaintance seems like an especial friend, when we meet, away out here, so far from home, or anywhere else.

PRAIRIE DOGS.

Tuesday, June 20.

Winthrop was quite sick last night with cramp colic. I was up with him the latter part of the night, so was dressed and ready for my visit to Prairie Dog Town at an early hour. The little fellows were up, standing at their doors, and greeted me with a welcoming bark. Some of them turned and darted away, no doubt to tell others we had come, for they immediately came back to peep out at us and bark and chatter, as if carrying on a lively discussion. They seemed perfectly fearless as long as we kept our distance, but if we tried to get a nearer view, they whisked away, and were gone in an instant; then they would send out two or three scouts, and if we had gone far enough away, they would come again to their doors. They have been well described by many writers. Cash and Frank joined me, while at Prairie Dog Town.

I rode horseback this morning, and Milt Walker rode with me. Winthrop is about well this evening. His was the first sickness we have had. Will Musgrove came up with us while we were halted for noon—his train is a short distance behind—he rode with me in the wagon all afternoon, and drove the horses, and mother rode Dick. We had a long talk about friends at home. He took dinner with us, and then said good-bye, and we will see him no more, for we will travel faster than the freight train.

*   *   *   *   *

Wednesday, June 21.

Mr. and Mrs. Morrison are large-hearted, cheerful people, who seem to be always happy and trying to make others happy. Mrs. Morrison learned that Miss Lyde Walker has her guitar, and sings beautifully, so she invited her to come to their tent and help to entertain a few friends. It was a very pleasant diversion. While Lyde was singing, the men and boys from all over the corral came near to listen. When she sang "The Cottage by the Sea," both inside and outside the tent, there was great applause that terminated in an encore. But no, she would not sing any more; she murmured something about the rabble, and laid her guitar away.

If I was gifted with a talent, with which I could give pleasure to people, I would certainly do so whenever opportunity was afforded. I would be glad to promote the happiness, and dispel as much sorrow as possible, in this sorrowful world.

159

Thursday, June 22.

We came through a place called Star Ranch, or Old California Crossing. We are camped twelve miles below Julesburgh. Mr. Reade called this evening; we told him we had decided to go to Montana. He seemed as pleased as though personally interested. Says the Irvine train is only half a mile ahead to-night, and invited us to go with him to call upon the young ladies. We, with one accord, asked to be excused. We all felt that we are not in calling costume.

*   *   *   *   *

Friday, June 23.

We are camping in Colorado. Came through Julesburgh, a rather insignificant-looking place, to have such notoriety as it has in the newspapers. We met a company of soldiers with about twenty Indian prisoners. They were captured at Fort Laramie, and they are taking them to Fort Kearney. The soldiers had a fight with about one thousand Indians three weeks ago. There were no soldiers killed, though a number were seriously wounded, and they lost a good many horses. There were squaws and papooses with the prisoners, though not captives.

The Indians in the fight were Sioux and Cheyennes; they all look alike to me. They were the most wretched-looking human creatures I ever saw, nothing majestic, dignified, or noble-looking about any of the Indians I have seen. An ex-Confederate soldier gave me my information about the fight. There are a great many

Southern soldiers on this route. We passed another newly-made grave this afternoon. Mr. Reade called this evening.

*   *   *   *   *

Saturday, June 24.

I was caught in a hail-storm this morning. I was half a mile from the wagons, on a high bluff, looking over the river, watching the storm coming. I did not realize that it was so near, but all at once it came down pell-mell and gave me some pretty hard knocks. Dick seemed in a hurry to get to the train, and I let him go. We seemed to fly over the ground through the storm, but we had the benefit of it all, for it stopped just when we reached the wagons.

I unsaddled Dick and turned him out, while I took passage in the wagon, changed my wet clothes for dry ones and wrapped in a shawl to keep from taking cold. When the teams were being hitched up at noon, Hillhouse said to me, "Dick has not had water; you would better ride to the river and give him a drink."

The river was half a mile from the road, but in sight all the way. Dick cantered to the watering place, drank all he wanted, and we started back when I saw someone coming toward me. I will not say who it was because of what followed.

"I thought you were getting too far behind for safety."

"Oh, there isn't any danger; you need not bother about me."

"Bother? Oh, no." And then came a declaration that about took my breath. At first I felt that I would like to box the presumptuous boy's ears. Then I wanted so much to laugh. But when I saw how desperately in earnest he was I thought, perhaps, I have been to blame for not seeing how things were tending. I was perfectly amazed; such a thought never occurred to me.

Our ride back to the train was rather embarrassing to me. I tried to make him see the comicality of the whole business, but he would not see it. We passed a station where the Indians had burned all that would burn, but these adobe, dirt-roof houses, or cabins rather, would not make much of a blaze I imagine. Inside one of the cabins—or what was left of it—were two dead Indians that had been killed in the fray.

*　　*　　*　　*　　*

Sunday, June 25.

Mr. Reade came with six young ladies to call upon us this morning, also one gentleman from the Irvine train. They had gone down into their trunks and were dressed in civilization costumes. They were Misses Nannie and Maggie Irvine—sisters—their brother, Tom Irvine, Miss Mollie Irvine, a cousin—Miss Forbes, and two other young ladies, whose names I have forgotten. They are all very pleasant, intelligent young people.

The trains are keeping as close together as possible, for protection, for the Indians are on the warpath. Every station and ranch-building that we are passing these days have been destroyed.

PREACHING SERVICES.

We have had a preaching service this afternoon. Rev. Mr. Austin, of the Methodist-Episcopal Church South—the church that I am a member of—was the preacher. The services were well attended, and the sermon was fine. He compared our situation with that of "The Children of Israel" in the wilderness. He spoke of God's care for them, and that He careth for us, spoke in an earnest manner of our dependence upon God, and our inability to take care of ourselves, or to accomplish anything without God's help and co-operation, and of the necessity of earnest prayer and faith in all circumstances of life, and always to remember that "The Everlasting Arms are underneath."

When the people were gathered, at the call of the bugle, some sat on chairs in the shade of wagons, some under umbrellas, some in carriages and light wagons. Mother and I stood near a carriage, before the service commenced, when a lady invited us to sit with her and her children—a little boy of five and a girl of three. We accepted and were introduced to Mrs. Yager, wife of the physician for the Chilicothe train, Mr. Dickerson captain. The services were held at their camp. Mrs. Yager is a Southern Methodist, too. Rev. Austin is a member of the Chilicothe train. I am glad there is at least one preacher among us.

MUSIC IN CAMP.

Monday, June 26.

Mr. and Mrs. May—a newly-married couple that came into our train at the junction of the roads—are both musicians; several of our young men have fine voices, and with Lyde's guitar, and Mr. May's violin we have had an enjoyable musicale away out here in the wilderness. If the Indians had been within listening distance it would be interesting to know what impression the music made upon their minds, as "Music hath charms, etc." The music this evening has been the happiest feature of the day, for I have had to ride in the wagon all day. One of the big horses went lame this morning, so Dick was put in harness and the dear little fellow has worked all day. He looks funny beside the big horse; the harness had to be taken up to the last holes to make it fit him. I would not enjoy taking this trip without a saddle-horse or pony to ride. I must be more generous hereafter and let Lyde and Mrs. Kennedy and other ladies that have no horse ride Dick oftener than I have been doing. I have not fully realized how very tiresome it is to ride in the wagon all day, and day after day.

I have always supposed that good water would be very scarce on this road; we have not found it so, there are always from one to three wells at the stage-stations, with excellent water, free for all—thanks to Uncle Sam for this provision for our welfare. In some places wood is very scarce and must be hauled long distances; we cooked dinner this evening with wood hauled from near Cottonwood. Cedar logs are fastened under the wagons, lengthwise between the wheels; as there are no stumps or rocks in the road they carry all right, when there is no wood to pick up the log is taken down, a piece cut off and split up for use. It is surprising with what a little bit of wood one can cook a meal on these sheet-iron stoves.

Tuesday, June 27.

Among the men who are driving for the Walkers is an eccentric old bachelor named Fogy; he is very bashful when in the presence of ladies. I have often heard it said that men cannot drive oxen without swearing; it is a mistake. I have seen a whole lot of ox-driving on this trip, and to-day I heard the first profane oath since we left the Missouri River. It would have been funny if it had not been shocking. We have traveled all day where the bluffs come close to the river, the road is very uneven, little hills and hollows, in some of the hollows there is mud. Mr. Fogy admires Neelie very much (at a distance, of course), we often hear the extravagant compliments he pays her, and his regrets about that troublesome "if."

Soon after the start this morning, Neelie and I rode to the front to escape the dust and sand that were flying; as we came near the front wagon we were startled by hearing a terrific oath. The wagon had stuck in the mud and would, of course, stop the entire train. Mr. Fogy was the driver. He was greatly embarrassed and distressed when he knew we had heard him swear, and stopped stock still and let the wheels sink into the mud so that they had to double teams to get them out. He afterward told some of the boys he was effectually cured of swearing; that he never felt so cheap in his life, and if he is ever tempted to swear he knows the remembrance of that moment will check him.

We had a refreshing shower about two o'clock, that laid the dust, cooled the air, and made everything sweet and fresh. We hoped and expected to have a pleasant afternoon, after the rain there was a calm—not a little tiny breeze or breath of air—it was just suffocating, and then came a cloud of buffalo-gnats that almost devoured us, so that horseback riding was an impossibility.

*　　*　　*　　*　　*

Wednesday, June 28.

Cash is on the sick-list to-day. I trust it will not prove to be anything serious. I greatly fear Mr. Kerfoot's family are destined to have considerable sickness before this trip is ended. They have such a sameness of diet, and it is so poorly cooked I fear the result.

When we started on this trip not one member of the family had ever prepared an entire meal; they had always had a houseful of servants to cook and do everything else for them. The first two or three weeks Neelie and her mother tried to learn to cook, and mother and I tried to teach them. It takes great patience to learn to bake in stoves out of doors; they heat red-hot so quickly, and cool just as suddenly; they must have careful attention all the time.

They made several failures baking light bread, and, giving it up in disgust, settled down to biscuit, that are hard as brick-bats, when cold, bacon, coffee, and beans—when we stop long enough to cook them. They were well supplied with fruit at first; the canned fruit was so easily served that it is all gone. They have dried fruit, but think it too much trouble to cook. Neelie does the cooking with some assistance from her father, such as getting wood, making fires, bringing water, grinding the coffee, etc. Henrietta and Emma—the next younger sisters—wash the dishes. It is no small undertaking to cook for a family of twelve; I do not blame Neelie for getting tired, she says they have such appetites it is not worth while to tempt them with extras.

Neelie is the dearest, sweetest, most unselfish daughter and sister; it seems they all depend upon her, the children go to her in their troubles and perplexities, her father and mother rely upon her, and she is always ready to do what she can for any and everybody that needs her help; she is unselfishness personified.

The wind blew so all afternoon that we could not ride horseback. The roads are smooth and hard as asphalt, result of rain yesterday and the wind to-day. Dr. Fletcher who was called to prescribe for Cash says she will be all right in a day or two.

THE MOUNTAINS IN SIGHT.

Thursday, June 29.

We could see the mountains, as the sun was sinking behind them; they were plainly visible though one hundred miles away. It does not seem possible they are so far away. Long's Peak and others near it are the points in sight. They look very much as I have imagined mountains would appear in the distance.

Mr. Walker is my informant as to names of places, distances, etc. He has been over the road and seems to know all about it. We usually ride some hours in company each day, so I have fine opportunities for asking questions, and he seems a willing instructor. He never broaches the sentimental, has never paid me a compliment in words I am glad to say, for since my late experience I would hesitate to ride with him were he not the sensible man that he is. We crossed a small stream to-day that was bridged and had to pay fifty cents toll for each wagon; the ford had been spoiled, or we could have crossed without the bridge.

*　　*　　*　　*　　*

Friday, June 30.

We stopped at noon where the road forks, the left-hand road goes to Denver. Mr. and Mrs. May, and Mr. and Mrs. Kirkland and children took the left-hand road, as they are going to Denver. Mr. May's brother, George, goes on to Montana on horseback; he will leave us in the morning and depend upon reaching stations, or emigrant camps, for food and shelter nights. I do hope the Indians will not get his scalp.

We have been feasting on antelope, the first that any of our party have killed. It is fine, much better than venison—but then I never ate venison when I was so hungry for fresh meat—we do get so tired of cured meat. We see no game except antelope and jack rabbits. The great herds of buffalo—that we read about—have not been in sight as yet.

Mr. Morrison's four-horse team ran away this afternoon with Mrs. Morrison and the children in the wagon. I had been riding with them since noon, had just left the wagon. When all the horse teams were driven out of ranks and down to the river for water, the lead horses took fright at an ant-hill—the ant-hills are big as a chicken-house—and started to run. There were several men near who caught and stopped them just as the forewheel went over the bank of the river. Mr. Harding was driving; he tried to rein them away from the river but they were right on the verge when stopped, one moment more and there would have been a serious accident. Mrs. Morrison did not scream nor try to jump out, neither did she allow the children to, but sat quite still and acted like the sensible woman that she is.

We are only six miles below the crossing of the South Platte.

*　　*　　*　　*　　*

Saturday, July 1.

We were awakened this morning at the first peep of dawn by the sound of the bugle call. Soon the teams were hitched, corral broken, and we were journeying to the crossing of the river, where we were driven into corral again. While we were getting breakfast the men were raising the wagon-beds and fixing them upon blocks as high as the wheels, and binding them tight with ropes to the coupling poles and lower parts of the wagons, ready to ford the river. They had a top-heavy appearance, as if the least jolt would topple them over. Some of the women were very nervous about riding in wagons set up on stilts, and felt quite certain somebody would be drowned. Wagons were crossing when we drove into corral, of course we had to wait our turn— first come, first served. Some enterprising young men have the blocks and ropes there to rent, at a very reasonable hire, too, for they might have asked what they would, we had no choice but to use them.

The river is half a mile or more wide, about half way over there is a large freight wagon stuck in the quicksand, just below the track of the wagons; it has been there since yesterday; it is slowly, slowly sinking, and cannot be gotten out. It has been unloaded and left to its fate, it seems a signal of distress to warn drivers to keep farther up the river and avoid the quicksands.

I drove the horse team over, and Hillhouse rode Dick and directed our going. The wagons of our train were all over and in corral by two o'clock without accident or mishap. Wagons have been crossing all day, and this evening we are a considerable town of tents and wagons; more than two hundred wagons within sight on the north side of the South Platte, at the eastern extremity of Fremont's Orchard—though why it is called an orchard I cannot understand, for there is certainly no fruit, neither promise of fruit about it, mostly quaking-asp and cottonwood, I think. Our corral is just to the left of where the wagons drive out, and near the bank of the river. Hillhouse has crossed the river on Dick at least twenty times to-day; he seemed to know just how to help and has been in constant demand, so he and Dick are thoroughly tired out to-night. We will stay here over Sunday, and hope to have religious services to-morrow as there are several preachers with us. I have not met any of them except Brother Austin who preached for us last Sunday.

Cash is much better, able to be out, though quite pale and weak. The mountains looming up in the distance seem to be the goal to which we are tending, and now we seem to make some progress every day for we are certainly nearer than when we first saw them on the twenty-ninth of June. Before they came in sight we did not seem to make any progress, but traveled day after day, and seemed to camp at night always in the same place; there was such a sameness in the landscape. In the early morning when the sun shines upon the snow-capped mountains the effect is thrilling; they seem to be the great altars of earth raised up to Heaven for the morning sacrifice.

A TOWN OF TENTS AND WAGONS.

Sunday, July 2.

It is wonderful, wonderful to behold how this town of tents and wagons has sprung up since yesterday morning when there was no sign of life on this north bank of the South Platte, and now there are more than one thousand men, women and children, and I cannot guess how many wagons and tents. The wagons have been crossing all day, the last one has just been driven into corral at sunset.

I was sitting on the bank of the river watching with anxiety the wagons as they ploughed through the deep waters—for the ford has washed out and the wagons go in much deeper than when we crossed yesterday— when a gentleman came and introduced himself as Dr. Howard, physician for the McMahan train. He said, "Miss Raymond, I have known you by sight since we camped at Kearney, and now as I have an errand for an excuse I hope to become better acquainted."

I could not imagine what his errand could be, for he talked of other matters for fifteen minutes or more, then said, "Miss Raymond, I have been directed to your wagons for the best and most wholesome bread that is baked on this road. Captain McMahan's nephew,

Robert Southerland, has been very sick but is now convalescing and needs nutritious and wholesome food to help him gain strength. I came to ask you for a piece of good bread."

Of course I gave him a loaf, and said, "Come get more when that is gone." He thanked me profusely.

There has been no serious accident nor any lives lost, although thousands of cattle, hundreds of horses, and more than a thousand human beings have crossed the river since yesterday morning.

Oh, for the pen of a Dickens to describe this wonderful scene, which no one ever has or ever will see again, just as it is. The moon is at the full and shining brightly as there is not a cloud in the sky, the camp-fires do not glow as they do dark nights. The men are building a great bonfire in the middle of our extemporaneous town.

WE WORSHIP IN THE WILDERNESS.

There is to be a praise and thanksgiving service for our safe conduct through the deep waters and our protection from the Indians. The people are beginning to gather near the bonfire and I must go, too.

*   *   *   *   *

Later.

Our service is over; it was grand, the singing of the old familiar hymns by so many voices spontaneously was inspiring, the talks by five or six ministers of different denominations were full of love for the Master, and brotherly love for every one.

172

An invitation was then given for all who had enlisted in the service of the Master to come forward and shake hands with the preachers, thus testifying for Christ. Neelie was the first one in that long procession to give her hand. Precious girl, she is always first in every good work. I noticed Dr. Howard in line, and I also noticed that Mr. Reade and Milt Walker were not among the soldiers of the cross.

The feed for stock is abundant, if it were not so, all these cattle and horses could not find pasture.

*　　*　　*　　*　　*

Monday, July 3.

The scenes in this great expanse of low, level land on the north side of the Platte in the early hours of this morning is hard to describe. Corrals and camps here, there and everywhere. Cattle and horses being driven into corrals to be harnessed and yoked, men and women cooking by camp-fires and on stoves, everybody seemed to be in a great hurry, all was animation and life, men riding after horses, oxen and mules; yelling, hallooing and calling, but not a profane oath did I hear. Among so many children, we rarely ever hear a child cry, and never hear a woman scold.

Our train was the third to break camp and file into the road this morning. The place that knew us yesterday will know us no more forever. Our town of tents and wagons that was teeming with life this morning is this evening deserted, silent, and uninhabited. We have folded our tents and driven or rode away. I did not mount immediately, but led Dick by the bridle, and gathered a magnificent bouquet of the most beautiful wild flowers. I had loitered by the way and did not notice that I was getting far behind our train, when I looked up and saw only strangers in the train that was passing. I thought it was time to mount, threw the bridle over Dick's head, while arranging my flowers, so that I would not crush them. I saw a gentleman in the train throw down his whip and start toward me, as if to assist me in mounting. I waited until he was quite near, then placing a hand on either horn I sprang lightly into the saddle, turned and waved my bouquet toward him as Dick galloped off. Such a cheer as the men in the train did raise, and then such merry laughter; it was fun to hear them.

Dr. Howard says it was Colonel Woolfolk—a gallant young widower—and the men that witnessed it guyed him unmercifully on having been snubbed. We came to the western extremity of Fremont's Orchard, ten miles, and stopped for lunch. Then came the Sand Hills, where all the heaviest wagons had to double teams to get through. The captain came on four miles and selected a camping ground, and we drove to our places, to wait for the heavy wagons to get through the sand.

Hillhouse, and several others, who came on with us, went hunting for antelope. We have been feasting on antelope for several days; it is fine, but if I could have my choice I would rather live on ham and bacon all the while than to have our men go hunting in this Indian country. Since we have crossed the Platte we have no protection from the soldiers, as there are no stations on this side the river.

We suffer agony when our boys are away from camp guarding stock or hunting. I have no fears for myself

174

nor any of us while we are all together in corral; but just a few away by themselves, how easily they might be cut off. There were Indians seen this morning by men looking for feed for the stock. It is almost dark and the boys have not come. I think the captain is getting anxious; he keeps looking in the direction the boys have gone. Ten P.M. The boys have just come with one antelope. They lost their bearings and came to the river, one mile or more above camp, and that was what kept them so late. When we scolded, they said they were obliged to stay to get at least one antelope for our Fourth of July dinner to-morrow.

WE CELEBRATE THE FOURTH.

Tuesday, July 4.

We made corral at eleven A.M., the captain announcing, "That we will stay four hours." I do not know if we stopped so soon, because it is the Fourth, or because it is so intensely warm, and the sun beams so hot, or because it was such a delightful camping-place. Whatever the cause, there we rested beneath the shade of large cottonwood trees, and it was so pleasant.

We had dinner at two. Our bill-of-fare—oyster soup, roast antelope with oyster-dressing, cold beans warmed over, dried fruit sauce, and our last cake and custard for dessert. We used the last of our eggs, which were packed in salt; it is surprising how nicely they have kept. I believe they would have kept another month. We had a very enjoyable feast, with an abundance of lemonade without ice. The boys put up a large swing on two large cottonwood trees; two could swing at once, with lots of strong arms to send us away up high. We began to file into the road at three P.M. Our fun was all too short. Dr. Fletcher rode with Neelie, and Milt Walker with me.

*   *   *   *   *

Wednesday, July 5.

Here is where we would have crossed the South Platte—if we had not forded it at the east end of Fremont's Orchard—on Lathan's Ferry. If all those wagons had crossed on the ferry it would have been a big pile of money for the ferrymen, for they charge one dollar a team.

We passed a squalid-looking Indian village to-day; it was just teepees and huts. Oh, dear, but they do look so uncomfortable. We are at the mouth of the Cache la Poudre—where somebody cachéd their powder. The water is so very clear and cold; it seems so nice after the muddy Platte. As there are no stations on the north side of the river, there are no wells. The Cache la Poudre is supplied by springs that flow from the snow-capped mountains that seem to be right over there.

*   *   *   *   *

Thursday, July 6.

As we were passing another Indian town I peeped into two or three of their dwelling-places. They are desolate-looking homes; no sleeping-places, no tables, chairs nor any furniture, just some rolls of blankets and buffalo robes, some camp-kettles, and that was all. There were squaws and pappooses innumerable squatted around on the outside of their teepees, the squaws making moccasins, or decorating them with beads. When we said "How," they grinned and held up two fingers, indicating they wanted two dollars for a pair. We did not purchase.

THE BLACK HILLS.

Friday, July 7.

We are camped at the foot of the Black Hills. They seem like immense mountains to me. There are four large corrals near the little village of La Porte. We rushed through with dinner, then Mrs. Hardinbrooke and I started for the top, taking our note-books with us. Before we had gone far, Winthrop and Frank joined us. Frank brought his gun; I do not know if he expected to find Indians or antelope up here. After much puffing and blowing, climbing and clambering, we reached the top. Oh, it is magnificently grand. If only I could make a pen-picture of this scene that others might realize it, as I do.

The mount upon which we stand is shaped like the quarter of a ball or globe miles and miles in diameter and circumference; we having climbed up the outside of the quarter to the top edge are looking down a steep precipice—the perpendicular side of the quarter. When a stone is thrown over, it takes it twenty-five seconds to reach the bottom, where the Cache la Poudre River runs at the base of the precipice.

How easy to step off into eternity from this place. I would not like to live near here, lest I might be tempted to do it some time. The valley over there looks as if— away back in the ages past—another quarter of the great ball that had been separated from this quarter, had been lifted by giant hands and carried away, leaving the most picturesque valley that I have ever beheld. There are three prosperous-looking farms in sight, a large herd of cattle grazing, and a beautiful grove or park at the northern end of the vale. West of the valley, and opposite where we stand, are peaks much higher than this; behind which the sun is sinking. The setting sun has crowned the mountain-tops with a crown of glory and brightness. The moon is rising out of beautiful, white fleecy clouds in the east. It is lovely beyond description.

> *How beauteous is this earth,*
> *How bright the sky,*
> *How wisely planned by him*
> *Who reigns on high.*

The sun is gone, night is coming; we must go, for we are at least one and a half miles from camp. I fired Frank's gun before starting; I aimed at the river, and hit the mark. How weak and insignificant these words seem when compared with the reality.

WE VISIT A BEAUTIFUL SPRING.

Saturday, July 8.

The scenic beauty of the route we have come over to-day was ever changing. We were either coming through a narrow cañon, across a beautiful vale, climbing or descending a steep hill or mountain. Nellie Bower and I had started on horseback to have the morning to ourselves, when Mr. Walker rode up and asked us to go with him to a lovely spring of delightfully cold, clear water he knew of, some two or three miles ahead. We consented, of course, and had soon left the wagons behind us. Mr. W. has been over the road before and seems to know the landmarks and places of interest. We found the spring, as described, in a beautiful dell, where the loveliest wild flowers I ever saw are growing luxuriantly. We were soon off our horses, enjoying the cool, delicious spring water. We gave our horses a drink, and then we each gathered a large bouquet of beautiful, fragrant wild flowers. They certainly are "wasting their sweetness on the desert air."

I believe we were almost an hour ahead of the train. Mother scolded, and so did Mr. Bower, because we had gone so far ahead of the wagons, for it is said these hills are full of Indians. I am all the time forgetting about the Indians. Mr. Kerfoot will not allow his girls to get out of sight. I am glad mother is not so exacting as that, but I ought not to impose upon her good nature, and cause her to worry. I never do intentionally, but sometimes I forget.

We are camping in a beautiful basin surrounded on all sides by high hills, and where the grass is plentiful. There is only one other train with us, but then it is the McMahan train, and they are all such fine-looking young men—and of course they are brave—that I always feel safe when they are near. Our captain has forbidden our going out of sight of camp. There are cañons in all directions; how I would like to explore.

Hillhouse and Sim Buford gathered some wild currants while herding; they will pass for fruit, but they look better than they taste. We have made sauce of them; with lots of sugar and cream they look inviting, and the boys seem to like them; very few will satisfy me. We can always have cream for breakfast, as the milk stands over night, and a pat of the sweetest, most delicious butter every evening, when we travel, as the milk is churned by the motion of the wagon. Fruit is very necessary on this trip, because of the alkali in the water, dust, and air we breathe, to keep us in health.

*   *   *   *   *

Sunday, July 9.

I was up very early this morning; I cannot spend precious time in bed after daylight while we are camping in this delightful place and have this perfect weather. I led Dick to the spring for a drink, bathed my face and hands in the cool water, picked a bouquet for the breakfast-table, and returned to camp to find the girls in bed. They missed a glorious sight by not seeing the sun rise.

Mother and Mrs. Hardinbrooke went with me to the top of the hill nearest camp this afternoon. They picked flowers and enjoyed the view for a while, then returned to camp, leaving me to come later. I sat on a large flat rock, just below the top, as mother said, "The Indians could see me so much farther if on the very top." I promised her I would not go out of sight; that if an Indian carried me off they could see him and know where I had gone. I did so enjoy the quiet of this Sunday afternoon; I had Mrs. Prentiss's delightful book, "*Stepping Heavenward*," to read, and time passed so quickly the sun was setting before I thought of going back to camp. Some of the boys laughed and said, "We were watching, and if an Indian had put in an appearance we'd have settled him; we knew you would not see him until he had you." I thanked them for their watchfulness.

WE CUT OUR NAMES IN STONE.

Monday, July 10.

Just when we had mounted our ponies for our morning ride, Mr. Walker came and asked us to go with him to the top of a mountain we could see far ahead and to the right of the road. He said, "The prospect is very fine, indeed, from that mountain-top. I was there two years ago."

Cash and Neelie were included in the invitation, also Mary Gatewood, but their fathers would not let them go. So Nellie Bower and I were the only ones who were allowed to accept his invitation. We rode our ponies until the ascent became too steep, and then dismounted and climbed. It was a hard climb, but we were amply paid. The view was magnificently grand. We found Mr. Walker's name where he had cut it in the soft stone two years ago, and we left our names, with date and former place of residence, cut in the stone. There were hundreds of names there, but I looked in vain for a familiar one. I wonder if any one that we know will find ours? We passed the graves of two men this morning who had been killed by the Indians. What a sad fate; God forbid that any of our men or boys should die such a death.

We are camping near a military post—Virginia Dale. It is just as beautiful as the name would imply. There are soldiers here for the protection of emigrants passing through these hills and mountains. Cash and I were riding with the captain when we came to the station.

The officer in charge came out to speak to the captain and asked some significant questions, "How long have you been in the hills?"

"Two days and nights."

"Where have you camped?"

"In that basin about eighteen miles back. We stayed over Sunday."

"Have the Indians troubled you?"

"We have seen no Indians."

He seemed greatly surprised, and said, "There has been no train come over that road within the last month without trouble, especially where you stayed over Sunday. Did not you notice those cañons in every direction? The Indians could surround you before you could know there was one near. The hills are full of Indians."

He told the captain where to camp, and where to send the stock for safety and protection. The captain thanked him, and we were starting on when the McMahan train came in sight.

"Ah, ha!" he exclaimed, "I see now why you have not been molested. Just keep that train in sight, and you need have no fear of Indians." And he just doubled up laughing until it was embarrassing to us.

"But why? Why will that train be a protection more than another?"

"Don't you see that portable engine lifted away up there, and all those iron pipes? The Indians think it is cannon, or some sort of machinery invented for their destruction; no doubt they believe it could kill them by the hundreds, though the mountains stood between it and them."

So that is why we have not been molested. We have heard of depredations before and behind us, but we have not seen an Indian. Blessings on the McMahan train; I hope we will not lose sight of it while we are in this Indian country.

We have passed through some very narrow cañons to-day, where there was barely room for one wagon to pass. Great rocks were hanging overhead on one side, with a rushing stream beside and just below the road on the other. There are beautiful waterfalls in the cañons. I was standing watching one of the highest, waiting for the wagons to pass. The last one had gone when Mr. Morrison came and peremptorily commanded me to "Come on, Miss Sallie. The I-I-I-Indians will c-c-c-carry you off some of these days," he stuttered. Of course I went.

The captain's orders are, "Do not leave camp this evening." We were only just corralled when I saw Lyde Walker climbing a near-by mountain. It is the first time I have known her to leave camp since we came into the Black Hills; she is very much afraid of Indians. When she came back I asked, "Why, Lyde, did you not hear the captain's order that we were not to leave camp this evening?"

"Oh, there is no danger when the men are on guard and watching. It is when they feel secure and are not looking out for them that I am afraid. Indians do not molest people when they are expecting them."

LARAMIE PLAINS.

Tuesday, July 11.

The sounding of the bugle and the echo that reverberated through the mountain gorges this morning was enchantingly sweet, and must have driven slumber from every eyelid. We left the hills at noon and are camping on Laramie Plains. We came over some very steep, rocky roads before we reached the plains. I watched the wagons anxiously as they descended the steep, rocky mountain-side, bounding and bumping against the big rocks, expecting and dreading an upset, but all landed safely on level ground at last, and I gave a sigh of relief and thanksgiving. We have not had an uncomfortably warm night all Summer, but while we have been coming through the hills the nights have been really cold, so that we have slept under blankets and comforts, like Winter-time. There is no sickness in camp at all; it is marvelous how very well we are. I hope it will continue so.

*   *   *   *   *

Wednesday, July 12.

We crossed the Big Laramie River just before noon. Had a good crossing; the water is clear, the bed of the river is covered with gravel, the banks are low, and the water is not very deep. I rode across on Dick; the water just came to my stirrup. We will stay here until to-morrow, as there is no water for fifteen or twenty miles, and we cannot go so far in half a day. We young people planned a fishing expedition for this evening, but the mosquitoes are so thick on the bank of the river we had to give it up. Some of the boys went seining; Brother

Winthrop was among them, so we will have fish for breakfast to-morrow morning.

The mosquitoes have not disturbed our rest at night, yet they have several times been very thick on the banks of the rivers, but have not been troublesome in camp. Perhaps the smoke keeps them away. The McMahan train keeps with us, so we are safe. Dr. Howard rode with us this morning; he is a widower.

*   *   *   *   *

Thursday, July 13.

We passed two large ponds of alkali this morning. The water had dried up, and the alkali was two or three inches thick all over the pond; it looked like ice, until we came very near.

Mrs. Hardinbrooke had a sick headache this afternoon; I took care of little Annie that she might not disturb her mother. She is a dear, sweet child and seems fond of me.

There was a rather serious accident as we were driving into corral. Mr. Hazelwood's horses were frightened and ran away, upsetting the wagon and smashing it up considerably. Mrs. Hazelwood, her sister, and two children were in the wagon; Mrs. H. was considerably bruised, the others were not hurt.

Dick drank alkali water this evening. I have been feeding him fat bacon; no doubt the grease and alkali have turned to soap before now in his stomach, and soap is not poison, so he will not die this time, and I will take better care of him the next time we are near alkali.

IN THE RAIN.

The men were until almost noon repairing the broken wagon. An accident that happens to one is assumed by all until results are overcome. As we were ready for the start, a little girl ran among the oxen to catch her pet crow; an ox kicked her on the forehead and cut a gash that had to have a few stitches and be bandaged, so we were delayed again. When order reigned once more we crossed the Little Laramie. It is very much like the Big Laramie, only not so wide nor deep; I rode Dick over, and then came on ahead of the train, keeping within sight. When we had traveled about an hour the rain came down. I was likely to get very wet before our wagons came, for they were among the last in the train; I took the saddle and bridle off Dick, sat down on the saddle to keep it dry, and to wait for the wagon. I was resigning myself to a drenching when Mr. Grier, driver of the front wagon, came and spread a great big rubber coat over me, so that I was completely sheltered and was hardly damp when our wagons came.

Then mother drove the horses close up to the wagon in front. I tossed my saddle and bridle in, hopped up on the tongue of the wagon before the wagon behind got close up, and we started without stopping but the one wagon. We could not stop until we came to feed for stock, so we were obliged to travel in the rain. We drove into corral about four P.M., and are again quite near the mountains. There are more pleasant things than camping in the rain. The water is so impregnated with alkali I fear it will cause sickness; the stock are in greater danger than we, for we can guard against it.

Saturday, July 15.

As I climbed out of the wagon this morning I saw the most beautiful rainbow I ever looked at. The bow was complete, the colors dazzlingly bright and just as vivid in the center as at the ends. It was not raining in camp, but raining hard on the mountain-side. The rainbow was so near we might easily have reached the end and "found the pot of gold." The rain came down all morning; we did not break camp until ten o'clock and then made only a short drive. We are camping among the hills once more, with not another train in sight. The McMahan train is behind us, but we do not know how far away they are, so we are glad to wait until they catch up. There is a mountain near that I would like to climb, but it is against orders.

*   *   *   *   *

Sunday, July 16.

We are all here; although some of the women last night seemed to think there was small chance of our seeing the light of this morning's sun. Had we known that the McMahan train was within calling distance—just a hill intervening—perhaps we would have rested easier and slept more soundly. It is considered a very dangerous place where we were last night and where we have traveled to-day. Although it is Sunday, I am sure there is not one in camp that would have voted to stay there to rest. We have heard horrible stories of the depredations that have been committed along this road and in these mountains within the last month. We saw with our own eyes—just before we came to Rock

Creek—a station that had been burned and all the inmates killed or taken prisoners; there were none to tell the story of the fight, although the bodies of all who were known to be there were not found. The buildings were not all burned, the fire either went out, or was put out by the rain, after the Indians left. They have been repaired, and soldiers stationed there now. We saw at the same station a coach that had been riddled with bullets; it was found on the road about a mile from the station, without horses, driver or passengers.

INDIANS.

It is supposed the Indians killed the driver, took the horses, and it is not known yet whether there were passengers or not, the coach being so riddled with bullets; it is feared there were passengers. A guard of soldiers go with the coaches we meet, or that pass us now. We crossed Rock Creek on a toll-bridge, and had to pay fifty cents toll for each wagon.

Just after we crossed the bridge, and where there is a sudden turn in the road, as it winds around the mountain, we saw where two men had been killed and two wagons burned last week. The tire became loose on a wheel of the next to the last wagon in a freight train, the men stopped to tighten it, while the rest of the train moved on, not thinking of danger, and was out of sight in a few minutes. An hour later some of the men came back to see what kept them. There they were—dead and scalped—the horses gone, and wagons on fire. The Indians had taken all the freight they could use, piled wood under the wagons, and set it on fire. We saw quantities of white beans scattered over the ground, also the irons from the wagons.

We are within sight of Elk Mountain and seemingly quite near it. Sim and Hillhouse picked a nice lot of gooseberries while stopping at noon. I have been sitting in the wagon, picking off stems all afternoon; they also brought a bucket of snow. It is really refreshing, and such a novelty to have a snow-ball to eat in July. The gooseberries are quite plentiful around here. Cash and I went with Hillhouse and Sim to pick some this evening, but a shower drove us to camp; the boys stayed and picked as long as they could see. If we had time, we could gather gooseberries enough to supply the train for a month. They are very fine and large; they are certainly an acceptable addition to our bill-of-fare, where a sameness of diet is unavoidable. I shall always consider them a fine fruit hereafter.

About an hour after we drove into corral the McMahan train came, and their corral is quite near. We are so glad they are here; we feel safe when they are near.

*   *   *   *   *

Monday, July 17.

Such a cold, rainy, dismal day as this has been. It has rained without stopping from early morn until now, and it is almost sundown. This is the first all-day rain we have had this Summer. It has rained all night several times, but that is not so bad.

Since we have been in this Indian country the tents have not been put up; every one seems to think it safer in the wagons than in tents outside the corral, so we have had to sit in the wagons all day. I have read, sewed, written, picked over gooseberries and ran through the rain and visited some, yet the day has seemed long. The herders have to take the stock two miles away to find feed, so we are consumed with anxiety, notwithstanding we know our Father's care is round and about us, and He can and will protect us. When we came here we could see Elk Mountain, but now it is enveloped in clouds, entirely hidden from view. It is not pleasant camping when it rains all day long.

*   *   *   *   *

Tuesday, July 18.

The wagons started soon after daylight, before we were out of bed. We had been on the road a little while when I heard Hillhouse call to Brother Winthrop—who was driving our wagon—"Oh, just look, Wint. Isn't that a grand sight?"

I knew there was something to see, so I was soon up and dressed and sitting with Winthrop. I shivered with cold until my teeth chattered, but was well repaid for any inconvenience by the grandeur of the sight I looked upon. Why try to describe or picture anything so entirely impossible? The masses of fleecy white clouds, with the brightness of the morning sun shining upon them as they floated around and over the top of the mountain, made an ever-changing, beauteous panorama that I cannot describe. As the clouds rose higher and higher, they seemed to mass over the top of the mountain, as in benediction, glittering in the sunshine until they seemed to melt away. I waited until the sun had warmed the air, then mounted Dick for my morning ride. The McMahan train broke corral and

190

drove into line just behind our wagons. I had only just started when Dr. Howard rode up on his pony Joe and requested the pleasure of riding with me. The doctor is a very pleasant, cultured gentleman, and is very fond of his pony, yet Joe cannot be compared with Dick for beauty, neither for easy gait. Why, Dick is the most beautiful pony on this road. He is a bright bay with long and heavy black mane and tail, and his gait is as easy as a cradle. I can ride all day and not be tired at all. While his horse—well, I will not describe him. It might hurt the doctor's feelings.

We came to the foot of Elk Mountain, on the Medicine Bow, about nine o'clock. We find plentiful and excellent feed for the stock, so the captains have announced, "We will stay here until to-morrow."

WE CLIMB ELK MOUNTAIN.

The doctor thanked me for the pleasure our morning ride had afforded him, and asked, "Can we not make up a party to climb Elk Mountain after breakfast?"

"I hope so. I will ask some of the young people."

About ten o'clock a few of us commenced the climb. Lyde Walker, Nellie Bower, Cash and Neelie, Sim Buford, Brother Hillhouse, Dr. Howard and myself. We were well paid for the effort; we found beautiful wild flowers, and some wild strawberries not five feet from a snow-bank. The snow is in a ravine on the north side where the sun does not shine. The berries and flowers are on the bank of the ravine, high enough to catch the rays of the sun, facing the south. The view was fine; we could see a large white lake far away to the west. Dr. Howard said it was alkali.

*   *   *   *   *

Wednesday, July 19.

We passed the alkali lake this afternoon. It was a strangely beautiful sight—the water as white as milk, the grass on the border intensely green. I always thought grass would not grow where there is alkali, but it is certainly growing there; the contrast of white and green was vivid. The wind was blowing the water into little glittering, dancing skipping wavelets; the sight was so unusual that it was fascinating, though the water is so dreadfully poisonous.

There are several musicians in the McMahan train; Lyde says they serenaded me last night. She says they stood between our two wagons. I think she is trying to tease me.

"Ask Dr. Howard, if you do not believe me. He was one of them."

"Oh, no. I would be ashamed to acknowledge I did not hear them, and would feel like a dunce if they had not been there."

Dr. Howard gave me the bouquet he gathered on Elk Mountain, which was most beautifully arranged, and asked me "To keep it until it falls to dust." I have put it between the leaves of a book and will perhaps never think of it again.

We came through Fort Halleck to-day. There were eight wigwams, or teepees, at the east end of the town; the squaws wore calico dresses and hoops. I believe they were more comical-looking than in their blankets. I fail as yet to recognize "The noble red man." They are anything else than dignified; they seem lazy, dirty, obnoxious-looking creatures.

Cash and I made a few purchases at Fort Halleck. I paid eighty cents for a quire of writing paper, and Cash paid fifty cents for a can of peaches. Mrs. Morrison is on the sick-list to-day, and Delia Kerfoot has a very sore mouth—scurvy, the doctor says, caused by the alkali in the dust and air. Neelie and Frank are both complaining.

WE CROSS THE NORTH PLATTE.

Thursday, July 20.

The ground was covered with a white frost this morning, and it is freezing cold. Mrs. Morrison and Frank are better; Delia's mouth is healing. Neelie continues to drag around; she will not acknowledge that she is sick enough to go to bed, but she certainly looks sick. I wish they would call Dr. Howard; somehow, I have more faith in him; perhaps because he is older and more experienced.

We are on the banks of the North Platte; arrived about three o'clock, did not stop for lunch at noon. We came ahead of the other trains, which will be here to-night. We will have the privilege of crossing first in the morning.

The men have taken the herds five miles away to get good feed. They are in danger from Indians. The captain called for volunteers. My brothers both offered to go, but the captain said, "Only one of Mrs. Raymond's boys must go."

Hillhouse said he would be the one. He was on guard last night, too.

We are in no danger here, for there are several trains here now and there will be more to-night. Oh, the anxious watching, the prayerful longing for day that we must endure this night, because of loved ones exposed to danger. What a precious privilege that we can go to the Mercy-seat with the assurance that if we ask aright our petitions will be granted. How do people live without Christ and a Mercy-seat? What can they do, when suffering anxiety, grief, or bereavement, if they cannot go to Jesus with their sorrows? Precious Saviour, what a refuge in time of trouble, what a joy to carry everything to God in prayer.

The McMahan train is near. Dr. Howard has been here; he begged me to let him see my diary. I asked to be excused.

*   *   *   *   *

Friday, July 21.

The night passed without alarm, and we are all here; I am thankful. Some of the men in our train were afraid to risk fording the river, and paid four dollars per wagon to be ferried over on a rickety old ferryboat that looked more dangerous than driving over.

Hillhouse and Winthrop were both engaged with the ox-team, Winthrop on the seat and Hillhouse riding Dick. When they drove into the river I motioned to mother to keep quiet and drove the horse-team right in behind them. The current is very swift; they had all they could do to keep the oxen from going with the current, and did not know I had followed them until they came out on an island in the middle of the river. Hillhouse smiled a sickly little smile, and said, "You should not have tried that."

Dr. Howard stood near, holding his pony by the bridle. He complimented me on my skill in driving, and said, "I saw you drive in that swift and treacherous river with bated breath, but soon saw that you knew what you were doing, yet I rode Joe in just behind you to be ready for emergencies."

"Thank you for your thoughtfulness. I will not 'halloo until I am out of the woods'—the other side is to be crossed yet."

Hillhouse said, "You would better wait on the island, and I will come back and drive your wagon over."

But of course I could not do that, after all the complimenting I had received. I drove in—with fear and trembling—for there lay a big freight wagon upset in the middle of the stream. It was more difficult than the first side, the banks higher and steeper, and the water deeper. We got over without mishap; the doctor came on his pony just behind us. I wandered off alone after lunch and climbed to the top of a near-by mountain. I found there a large pyramid of loose stones that looked as if they had been piled there by travelers, each one contributing a stone.

I selected a snow-white stone from the mountain-side and added to the pile. There is another town of wagons being made on the west side of the North Platte. The wagons have been crossing all day, and are crossing yet. Hundreds of wagons have been driven over that turbulent and rushing river, and not a serious accident occurred.

I have been on the lookout for the Irvine train, but it is not here. I think it is ahead of us, and we will not see the young ladies or Mr. Reade again on this trip, yet as we are all going to Montana we may perhaps meet again.

NEELIE IS SICK.

Saturday, July 22.

We are within sight of Pine Grove in Wyoming Territory.

Neelie was very much better this morning; almost well, she said at noon, and rode her pony this afternoon. I was riding with her when I noticed a heavy rain-storm coming. I begged her to come on and not risk getting wet.

"Oh no, Miss Sallie; I don't want to ride fast. This air is so delicious, and I think I want to ride alone for a while; you go on, and I will come very soon."

I saw it was useless to urge her. I am always careful not to expose myself unnecessarily to a drenching, so I raced on to our own wagons and had barely time to unsaddle Dick and turn him loose when down came the rain in torrents. I was so anxious about Neelie and expected her to come tearing through the rain. I looked from the back of the wagon and saw her coming— plodding along at the same slow gait, as if she did not know it was raining. When the rain was almost over she came along—drenched, of course. She laughed at my look of dismay and paid no heed to my scolding.

Mother and I both urged her to go quickly and change her wet garments for dry and warm ones. She got off her horse and climbed into the wagon. When we stopped I went around to see how she fared. She sat in the wagon with a blanket-shawl around her, and the wet clothes had not been changed for dry ones. She was shivering with cold.

"Oh, Neelie, my precious girl, I am afraid you have killed yourself."

"Oh, no, Miss Sallie; I am not so easily killed as all that."

"But, Neelie, you have been sick for a week, and now to get this drenching. I fear the consequences."

The family do not appear at all anxious, so there is nothing I can do but hope and trust that her naturally strong constitution may bear even this strain. I advised her to go to bed, drink hot tea, and get into a perspiration. I doubt very much if she will do it.

Milt Walker is on the sick-list, too. Hillhouse went to bed with a severe headache last night, but a night's rest has entirely restored him.

We crossed three very muddy streams to-day, the first muddy water we have seen since leaving the South Platte. Since coming to the mountains, the water has been as clear as crystal until to-day; perhaps we are coming into mining country. We stopped quite early this afternoon; the McMahan train has passed and gone out of sight. I hope they will not go too far, and that they will lend us protection with their portable engine and other machinery.

*   *   *   *   *

Sunday, July 23.

We are resting to-day. I went with Mrs. Hardinbrooke, Lyde and a gentleman friend of Lyde's, for a long ramble over the mountains this afternoon. We found a most delightful spring where the water seemingly gushes out of the rock. Just below this spring was a patch of the finest wild onions I ever saw. We brought a good supply to camp. We are so starved for green vegetables that everyone seems to enjoy the onions, though some had never eaten onions before, they said. For my part I always did like onions.

THE SUMMIT OE THE ROCKY MOUNTAINS.

Monday, July 24.

We passed the summit of the Rockies to-day, and are camping on the western or Pacific slope to-night. The ascent has been so gradual we should not have known when we reached the top but for the little rivulets running in different directions. Quite on the summit and very near to each other we saw two little rivulets starting on their way; one to meander toward the Pacific, while the other will empty its confluence into the Mississippi, and thence on to the Gulf. Just a scoopful of earth could change the course of either where they started—from the same spring really. As it is, how widely different the scenes through which they will pass. So it is with human lives—a crisis is reached, a decision is made, and in one short hour the whole trend of our life is changed with regard to our surroundings, associates, environments, etc.

We came through Bridger's Pass to-day, crossed a toll bridge near Sulphur Springs, and had to pay fifty cents toll for each wagon. The streams are all muddy that we have crossed to-day. We saw two beaver dams; they look like the work of man with shovel and trowel. We are camping two miles west of Sulphur Springs.

* * * * *

Tuesday, July 25.

We are camping near another muddy creek near a station that was attacked by Indians ten days ago; they wounded one soldier very severely and ran off with nine horses.

After we were in corral, while waiting for the stove to be set up and the fire to be made, I was sitting in mother's camp-chair idling and thinking, when Neelie came to me. She dropped upon the grass beside me and, laying her head in my lap, said, "Oh, Miss Sallie, I am afraid I am going to be sick in spite of everything, and I have tried so hard to get well without sending for the doctor."

Dr. Fletcher is desperately in love with her and tried to tell her so one day not long ago, catching her hands while talking, which she resented as a familiarity, and has not spoken to him since. She told me about it the evening after. It happened at noon. I told her I believed he was sincerely in earnest and that she had wounded him deeply.

She told me what she had done to try to cure herself; the medicine she has taken is enough to kill her. I called mother and told her what Neelie had told me.

Mother said, "You poor child, you do look sick, indeed; you must go to bed and send for the doctor right away." I went with her to the wagon, helped her to get ready for bed, and told Cash to send for Dr. Fletcher. She said she would as soon as Bush—her brother—came.

After dinner I went again to see Neelie; the doctor had not yet come, but Bush had gone for him. I stepped upon the tongue of the wagon and could, with difficulty, restrain an exclamation of disgust. Neelie interpreted my expression and said, "Cash just would do it; said I was looking so like a fright."

Cash had powdered and painted Neelie's pale face and crimped and curled her hair—and made her look ridiculous—trying to hide the sick look from the doctor. I did not answer Neelie, but went and scolded Cash; in a low tone she said, "She was so dark around the eyes, her lips blue, and her cheeks so pale I could not bear to have Dr. Fletcher see her looking so homely. She has told you about their little love-tiff?"

"Yes, but don't you suppose he can see through that paint and powder? I am afraid he will think Neelie did it, and she will appear ridiculous in his eyes." I saw the doctor coming, so came away. As I was sitting here writing, he came a while ago and said, "Miss Raymond, will you sit with Miss Kerfoot to-night and see that she has her medicine strictly at the right time?"

"Certainly I will. Is she very sick, doctor?"

"She is in a much more serious condition than she or the family realize. It would not be wise to alarm her, but the family ought to know she will need very careful attention. I will tell them to-morrow. You need not sit up after the last dose of medicine is given, which will be at midnight. I think she will rest better if everything is quiet, and the lights out."

I know from the doctor's tone and manner he thinks Neelie dangerously ill. The doctor gave me directions about her medicine, and I went immediately to her wagon.

SIM BUFORD SICK.

Wednesday, July 26.

Last evening as I was on my way to sit with Neelie I met Ezra. He said, "Miss Sallie, Sim is quite sick; very much like Cousin Neelie is, I think. I wonder if we are all going to be sick?"

"Oh, no; I hope not. I am very sorry Sim is sick."

When I left Neelie—a little after midnight—sleeping quietly, to come home, I noticed a light in the wagon that Sim and Frank occupy. I did not awake this morning until everything was ready for a very early start. Mother had kept my breakfast warm by keeping the stove until the last minute. I sat in the wagon and ate my breakfast after the train had started. When through I climbed out and went to see how Neelie was. I found her feverish and restless; her symptoms unfavorable.

Oh, the dust, the dust; it is terrible. I have never seen it half as bad; it seems to be almost knee-deep in places. We came twenty miles without stopping, and then camped for the night. We are near a fine spring of most excellent water—Barrel Spring it is called. I do not know why; there are no barrels there. When we stopped, the boys' faces were a sight; they were covered with all the dust that could stick on. One could just see the apertures where eyes, nose and mouth were through the dust; their appearance was frightful. How glad we all are to have plenty of clear, cold water to wash away the dust.

Neelie is no better. Such a long drive without rest and through such dust was enough to make a well person sick. I fear the consequences for both Neelie and Sim, for Sim is a very sick boy. Hillhouse told Sim last night that we would take him with us and take care of him, if he wanted to come and Mr. Kerfoot would let him. He wants to come, of course; so he sent for Mr. Kerfoot this morning to come to his wagon, as he wished to see him on business.

Mr. Kerfoot came, and Sim asked to be released from his contract to drive through to California. Mr. Kerfoot asked, "Why do you want to leave us?"

"I believe Montana is the place for a young man to go, and besides I am very sick and can have better care with the Raymonds than I can here, for Neelie needs all your attention."

"I reckon your chances are as good as the rest of us have." And walked off.

Frank came for me, and I went to see Sim; he is very sick, has a high fever and coated tongue. He asked me to see Mr. Kerfoot. Frank went with me. Mr. K. seemed to know what we came for; he was scarcely civil. I put the case plainly, and said, "We must take care of Sim, either with or without your consent; we owe it to his father and mother, and to himself, to see that he is taken care of. He cannot be taken care of where he is."

After re-arranging the boys' wagon and making room for Sim's bed and other belongings; Ezra, Frank and Hillhouse helped him to the wagon and put him to bed, while I went to the McMahan train, which was quite near, and asked Dr. Howard to come and prescribe for him. The doctor came, bringing the medicine with him. He says it is mountain fever.

OUR TRAIN DIVIDED.

The separation of the train is being talked of, and is no doubt absolutely necessary, for the herd is so large it is hard to find pasture for them all together. When the division is made, those going to California will form one corral, and those bound for Montana will form another. This will separate us from Mr. Kerfoot's family; I do hope we will not have to part while Neelie is so sick. I do so want to help take care of her.

*   *   *   *   *

Thursday, July 27.

Among the families that came into our train at Kearney was a family of four young ladies and their father—a widower—named Ryan. Sue, Kate, Mary and Maggie are their names. Mr. Ryan told some of the young men that he was taking his daughters to the west, where there are more men and fewer women, so they could have a better chance to get good husbands than in Missouri. It has been a good joke among the boys, and some of them have tried to be very gallant to the young ladies—as they are on the market.

George Carpenter, a driver for Hardinbrooke and Walker, when the train separated this morning, pretended to go into hysterics. He had a fit on the inside of the corral when Mr. Ryan drove off with the other half of the train. Mr. Kerfoot did not know he was fooling, and ran to his assistance; the captain passed, took in the situation and smiled. Mr. Kerfoot knew then it was a hoax, and it made him so mad he declared he would not stay in a train where the captain would smile at such conduct.

The doctor had said to him, "It is necessary that I see Neelie several times during the day, and you will be taking great risk if you leave the train until she is much better." He had decided to stay, and join the others any time before they came to the California road, west of Green River. He was so mad at the captain for smiling at Carpenter's nonsense, and because he did not rebuke him, that he made the boys bring in the horses and cattle and hitch up as quickly as possible. In an hour after the others started they had followed. Mr. Kerfoot did not say good-bye to any one. I do hope Neelie will not suffer for his crankiness.

We are now a corral of twenty wagons, the greater number freight wagons; they are in corral on the opposite side, while the families are all on our side. The Hardinbrookes, Walkers, Bowers, Kennedys, Morrisons, Currys—a family of five—Mr. and Mrs. Baily and their daughter, about ten years old, and a widowed sister of Mrs. Baily and her little girl, about the same age as her cousin, are with us at the back end of the corral. I do not know these people, only just to speak when we meet, but they now help to form our corral.

We came only two or three miles after the train separated, just far enough to get out of the dust. Mr.

Kerfoot's family and ours have been almost as one family since we have been on the road, and I have become greatly attached to all of them and especially to Neelie. She is the dearest, sweetest girl, so very unselfish, and always ready to help any and every one that needs help. There is not one in the family but could be spared better than Neelie except, of course, her father. They all love her so, and depend upon her for everything. She is a precious daughter, a darling sister, and a true friend.

Sim is very much better; he has some fever, but not so high a temperature as yesterday. Dr. Howard is very attentive. He says it is mountain fever that Sim and Neelie both have. Dr. Fletcher called him to see Neelie; he says she is a very sick girl, but not worse than Sim was when he first saw him. Her temperature is not so high.

I wonder if mountain fever is contagious, or what it is that causes it? It seems the air is so pure and invigorating one could not get sick at all. I never felt better in my life, and mother seems so well. I am afraid it is the sameness of diet and poor cooking that is making Mr. Kerfoot's folk sick. The bread they make is hard as brick-bats when cold.

WE OVERTAKE THE CALIFORNIA TRAIN.

Friday, July 28.

We came up with the other half of the train about ten o'clock, and have traveled in company the rest of the day. We have separate corrals about two hundred yards apart; the stock is not herded together.

Neelie has been restless with high fever and flighty when she dozes; with eyes half open, poor girl she is certainly very, very sick.

We are near a delightful spring, cold as ice, and clear as crystal. I went to the spring to bathe my face and hands, and brush my hair. Mr. Kerfoot and Frank came for water. Mr. Kerfoot said, "Miss Sallie, why don't you and your folks come and go to California, where you started to go?"

"Why, Uncle Ezra, you know the reason. We think Montana the better place for the boys to get a start, and we want to do the best we can for them."

"Tut, tut; wealth is not the chief thing in life. You can make a living anywhere, and Montana is an awful place. Why, the only law they have is mob law, and if a man is accused of crime he is hung without judge or jury."

"Notwithstanding, there seems to be a great many nice people going there, and I am not in the least afraid of my brothers being accused of crime."

"I do believe you will regret going to Montana, and I also believe it is all your doing that you are going. I think it is very unkind of you to leave us now when Neelie is so sick and needs you so much."

"We are not leaving you, Mr. Kerfoot; it is you leaving us against the doctor's orders, too."

I made a great mistake saying that, he fairly raved; he was so angry, actually beside himself with rage. He said very unkind things without the least foundation or truth in them, and which I will try to forget. I am so sorry for him. I did not answer a single angry word, and

I am glad I did not. But Frank did; he was about as angry as his uncle was, and talked manfully in my defense. He gave his uncle the lie, and clenched his fists and seemed ready to fight.

I ended the embarrassing scene by walking away. Mrs. Hardinbrooke was waiting for me; we climbed to the top of a very steep point, which was hard to climb, and we were out of breath when we reached the top and were glad to sit and rest. The view was fine, the evening pleasant, and we were glad of each other's companionship, but we did not talk. I think Mrs. Hardinbrooke attributed my silence to anxiety about Neelie, and she was not far from the truth.

* * * * *

Saturday, July 29.

Neelie was very much better this morning; her fever gone, she was very weak, but was free from pain. Her medicine had the desired effect. She had rested quite well last night—better than since she has been sick— and all her symptoms are favorable.

The doctor seemed greatly encouraged and told Mr. Kerfoot that if they would stay here until Monday he felt sure Neelie would be out of danger and they could move on without any risk of doing her harm. He did not dream that Mr. Kerfoot would again disregard his advice. Neelie continued better until noon, then some one proposed moving on a half day's drive, thought it would not hurt her if they made only short drives at a time.

Mr. Kerfoot listened, and finally consented. He is very much afraid of Indians, and in a few days we will be out of the Indian-infested country. The doctor is very much out of patience with him, told me he gave Mr. Kerfoot a piece of his mind.

You must make big allowance for the poor man. He does not realize that he is endangering Neelie's life; he cannot believe it possible that such a calamity as Neelie's death can befall them while he is trusting in a merciful Father above. Yet I do wish someone might have exercised authority and prevented their going.

Sim is very much better, improving rapidly. Mr. Walker is able to be around once more. I wonder if he had mountain fever?

I have been trying to get the dust out of our wagon this afternoon; it was hard work taking everything out and cleaning off the dust. Lyde Walker pleasantly entertained us this evening with songs accompanied with guitar. The wagon the Walkers occupy is just in front of ours since the separation.

ON BITTER CREEK.

Sunday, July 30.

We came fifteen miles to-day, but have not overtaken the California train. It must be that Neelie is no worse, and their traveling yesterday did her no harm, or they would have waited over to-day; we shall hope so anyway.

Dr. Howard rode with me this morning. We are traveling on Bitter Creek, which is considered the very worst part of all the road. I had heard so much about the desolateness of this part of the country that I expected to find a barren waste. It is not so bad as represented. There are long distances where there is not sufficient pasture for the stock, but in places the feed is plentiful. The captain and two or three men are off the road the greater part of the day hunting pasture; we stop when they find it at whatever hour it may be.

*　　*　　*　　*　　*

Monday, July 31.

We came twelve miles, passed one station; it was built of stone and seemed a very comfortable place. Mrs. Hardinbrooke has been quite sick to-day. I have taken care of little Annie. We have not had any word from Neelie. I trust that no news means good news. Sim was able to sit up in the wagon for a while this afternoon. I think with care he will be well in a few days. We have had delightful weather, since we passed the summit. The roads are quite dusty, but not like they were before we came to Barrel Springs. The water in Bitter Creek is not so nice as the mountain streams and springs, but it is not bitter, as I thought it would be from its name.

*　　*　　*　　*　　*

Tuesday, August 1.

We are at Point of Rocks, the place is rightly named; one who never saw them could hardly imagine such enormous piles of rock; they are high as mountains, with scarcely any dirt among them, the sides are smooth and even, the stone is soft like slate or sandstone, and the whole face of the enormous pile, as high as man can reach, is literally covered with names, dates, and places of former residence from all over the United States. I looked in vain for some familiar name. I left my name in a conspicuous place, so if any of my friends look for my name they will not be disappointed. There are springs flowing from the clefts in the rock; and oh, with what pleasurable anticipation did I hasten to partake of the pure water, as I, of course, supposed it was.

I had been riding with the captain as he came ahead to find a camping place when the train came. I rode to our wagon, got a cup and crossed Bitter Creek to get a drink of nice, cold spring water. I took one swallow. Oh, oh, oh; the horrid stuff. I was glad there was no one with me to see the face I made. I think I never swallowed a more disagreeable dose. It was the strongest sulphur-water I ever tasted. In my haste and eagerness I did not notice that the atmosphere was impregnated with sulphur, and the sulphur formations around the springs, because they were covered with dust.

The wind is blowing as cold as Greenland. I expect we will have to go to bed to keep from freezing. Mrs. Hardinbrooke is no better; her symptoms are the same as Sim's and Neelie's were at first, and we fear she is taking the fever. Dr. Fletcher thinks Neelie must be better, or we would have heard, as Mr. Kerfoot said he would send back for him if she got any worse.

DELAYED ANOTHER DAY.

Wednesday, August 2.

We had a very cold night; there was ice a quarter of an inch thick this morning. Several head of Hardinbrooke's and Walker's cattle were missing this morning; the men have been hunting them all day, they were found this evening in a cañon four miles from camp; there were the tracks of two horses, with shoes, that had driven them there. The Indians do not shoe their horses, so there must be thieves besides Indians in this country. And here we are another whole day's drive behind the other half of our train. Oh, I wonder if it will be possible to overtake them now, before our roads separate entirely. They must be at least two days ahead of us, if they have not been delayed.

*   *   *   *   *

Thursday, August 3.

The mountains in this region are very barren, composed of sand and rock, principally. It comes nearer being desert than anywhere on the road. We have traveled all day, and have come only thirteen miles. The road has been very rough indeed. I rode in the wagon the greater part of the day, so I could take care of little Annie Hardinbrooke; her mother is very sick. I have thought so much about Neelie, whenever the wheels would strike a rock, or jolt down into a rut; how she must have suffered, if in pain or fever; how hard it must have been for her.

Lyde says Dr. Fletcher is very impatient and cross, because of the delay; he threatened to take a horse and go horseback yesterday, when he found the train would not move. She thinks he is very anxious about Neelie, and very much in love.

*　　*　　*　　*　　*

Friday, August 4.

The wolves howled around our camp all last night and kept Cæsar—our watch-dog—barking; so we could not sleep. Have made only a short drive, and are camping at Rock Springs, where the road forks. The men are not agreed as to which road to take; the upper—or right-hand road—is the shortest, but the lower is best supplied with pasture and water. If we take the upper road we cannot hope to see our friends again, so Dr. Fletcher and I want to take the lower road, for we still hope that we may overtake them.

Mrs. Hardinbrooke is very sick; I fear we are going to have another case of serious sickness in our camp. I have taken care of Annie again to-day, which seems to be the most efficient service I can render, as Lyde and Mrs. Joe Walker take care of Mrs. Hardinbrooke when her husband cannot be with her. He takes all the care of her at night, and a most excellent nurse he seems to be. Sim is quite well, only pale and weak.

*　　*　　*　　*　　*

Saturday, August 5.

The decision was made in favor of the lower road. As the train was rolling out I had just mounted my pony, when Dr. Fletcher came and asked me to ride with him. He has never seemed to care for my

212

company, nor I for his until since we have been so anxious about Neelie. Our anxiety has been a bond of sympathy, and we have rather enjoyed each other's society. We had gone a short distance ahead of the train when we saw someone coming horseback. I soon saw that it was Frank. We hurried on to meet him. He shook hands without speaking. I asked, "How is Neelie?"

"She is very low. I came after you, doctor. Our camp is about four miles from here; we have waited two days for you, and thought you would certainly come yesterday. When you did not come, we thought you must have gone the upper road, and I was going back as far as the first station to inquire if you had passed. I am glad, indeed, to meet you, but greatly fear you will not be in time to save Neelie."

The doctor asked two or three questions, excused himself and rode away at a gallop, leaving Frank and I to follow, while I plied him with questions, which he answered patiently. He then said, "Neelie was much better for a day or two after we left you; we all thought she was getting well; she spoke of you every time I saw her, and wondered why you did not come. Since the fever came back I have not talked to her at all. Part of the time she has been delirious, and when conscious she was too weak to talk."

Oh, dear. I do so want to see her and help take care of her.

A FATAL SHOOTING.

We rode a while in silence, then Frank said, "That is not all the bad news I have to tell, Miss Sallie."

I looked up quickly and asked, "What else has happened, Frank?"

"Frasier was shot and killed day before yesterday evening."

"Oh, Frank; how did it happen?"

"Hosstetter did it, but I think he was not much to blame."

Frasier is the man who spoke to Cash, Neelie and I, as we were watching the wagons ferried across the Missouri River, whose son ran away from his mother, and home, to come to his father, and go with him to Montana. Frasier had teams and wagons for freighting, and Hosstetter some capital to invest in freight, to take to Montana. Frasier advised the purchase of flour, and he would freight it to Virginia City for fifteen dollars per cwt. He said flour was worth fifty and sixty dollars per hundred in Virginia City. (So it was in the Spring of 1864, and as high as seventy-five and one hundred dollars per hundred, which was the cause of a bread riot in Virginia City.)

No doubt Frasier was honest in his advice, and would have invested in flour for himself. He charged more freight than was right, for ten and twelve cents is the prevailing price; but then Hosstetter should have found that out for himself.

When he found he had been imposed upon and learned that flour is retailing at Virginia City for $15 per hundred, he was angry, dissatisfied, and perhaps quarrelsome. Frasier was no doubt very aggravating. They had quarreled several times, and the evening of the 3d, Frasier was heard to say to Hosstetter in a threatening tone:

214

"You may consider yourself lucky if you ever see Montana. You need not expect to get any of this flour. It will take it all to pay the freight."

It was getting dark, and Frasier stood with one hand on a wheel as he talked. He then got into the wagon and out again, with something in his hand, which Hosstetter thought was a revolver in the gathering darkness. He came back to the wheel where he had been standing when he made the threat, and Hosstetter thought he had come to shoot him, and fired twice, as he thought, to save his own life. Frasier fell, shot through the brain, and died instantly.

Then it was found he had a hatchet in his hand, and had come to tighten a tire on the wheel, which he had found loose when he laid his hand on it. Frasier's eldest son of fourteen years is here. There are five children and their mother at home. Hosstetter has three children and a wife. Eleven innocent persons to suffer, no one knows how intensely, for that rash act.

Frasier's son knelt beside his father's dead body, and placing his hand on his breast, he swore a fearful oath that he would have but one purpose in life until his father's death is avenged. Oh, what a shocking ambition for so young a boy.

Frasier and Hosstetter have traveled and camped near us all the way from Plattsmouth. When the train was organized they came into it; when it was divided they went with the others as there were not so many of them, and the herd was smaller.

By the time Frank and I had discussed the direful circumstances connected with Frasier's death, in the presence of this greater calamity Neelie's sickness did

215

not seem so sad an affliction as it had before, for she is not dead, and while there is life there is hope.

We came in sight of three corrals about eight o'clock, camping near together.

TRIED FOR MURDER.

Everything had a funereal appearance. Men stood around in small groups talking earnestly in a low voice, whittling sticks, the incessant occupation of most men when trying to think.

Those with whom we are acquainted bowed as we passed them, without speaking. I was soon off my horse and ready to see Neelie, while Frank took Dick to hitch him for me.

As I approached the tent where Neelie is, Mrs. Kerfoot came to meet me.

"How is she, Aunt Mildred?" I asked anxiously.

"We think perhaps she is better now. She is quiet and resting easy, but she has had a very restless night, and the doctor says she must be kept perfectly quiet; not the least excitement."

She had led me away from the tent while talking. I saw in a flash what she meant. I was *not* to see Neelie.

"After we left you she kept asking about you, and when you did not come, we thought perhaps you had gone the short cut, and so we told her you had gone the short cut to Montana, and we would not see you any more. She seemed grieved at first, but became reconciled to what could not be helped, and now, if she should see you of course it would excite her, and I know you would not do anything that might harm her, or make her worse."

"Oh, no; of course not."

Emma, Delia and Juddie had come to where we were talking. I kissed them all, said good-bye, and came away, with a heavy heart.

I unhitched Dick and, leading him by the bridle, went on in advance of the trains, selected a place for the corral, unsaddled Dick, and waited for the wagons. I did not have long to wait, and the captain was so good as to corral on the place I had selected.

I had a motive in being in advance of the other trains. I hoped to get Hillhouse and mother to consent to pull out of corral and go on if the train did not move. We are not in any danger from Indians now, and we can go alone if no others choose to go with us. I cannot bear to stay here and not see Neelie.

We could not move to-day, but Hillhouse says we will to-morrow morning. The men from these four trains elected judge, jury, prosecuting attorney and lawyer for the defense, and have tried Hosstetter for murder. The jury brought in a verdict of "Not guilty." He shot in self-defense, as Frasier had threatened to kill him.

Hillhouse served on a jury, the first time in his life. He is only twenty. They buried Frasier yesterday. Lyde and I visited his grave this afternoon. Hosstetter seems very remorseful; blames himself for being so hasty.

*　　*　　*　　*　　*

We were up bright and early this morning. By the time other camps were at breakfast we were ready to start, one other family with us, Mr. Curry, his wife and four boys. When Hillhouse spoke to the captain about our going on, he said he thought it advisable, as our teams are in good condition, the cattle not at all lame. We can make much better time than the train can, as so many of the cattle are lame, they will be obliged to travel slowly. There is no danger from Indians, and after we reach Green River pasture will be plentiful, without going away from camp to find it.

I climbed into Mrs. Hardinbrooke's wagon to tell her good-bye, kissed little Annie as she was sweetly sleeping. Mrs. H. seemed sorry to have us go. I met Dr. Fletcher as I was leaving Mrs. Hardinbrooke and asked about Neelie.

"She is very low, indeed. Of course, while there is life we may hope; but if she lives they will have to stay here a week or ten days."

I did not tell him we were leaving, but said good morning, and went to find Lyde. She was worried and anxious about Milt. He has been staying behind the train to drive lame oxen almost every day since he has been well enough. He is usually in camp by 10 P.M. Last night he did not come. She said, "Brother Joe is quite sick, too. I wonder what will happen next?"

"Oh, Lyde, no very serious calamity has happened to you or yours, nor me or mine. Let us not borrow trouble, but hope for the best. Milt will be here in a little while. I know he is able to take care of himself, and he is going to do it."

WE LEAVE THE TRAIN.

The wagons had started, so I mounted Dick and was off. As I came into the road I looked back, and saw Milt coming in sight, driving his lame oxen. I left the road once more and went to Frasier's grave. His son has set it with prickly pears, so closely that it will make a pretty mound if it grows, and will be a protection from wolves, unless their hides are thick and tough. Poor boy, he must have been seriously scratched while transplanting the prickly things, but perhaps it was a relief to his mental suffering, to bear physical pain while trying to do a last something for his poor father.

I spent a dreary morning. I feel the parting with our friends so distressingly. It is not likely we will meet again in this life. I think Sim is feeling blue over it, too.

We met a squad of soldiers from Green River going to arrest Hosstetter, and take him to Fort Bridger for trial. They say his trial was not legal. He and all the witnesses will have to go by the way of Fort Bridger, and will perhaps be detained for some time. I do hope for his own and his family's sake he will be cleared. The upper road from Rock Springs goes by the way of Fort Bridger, I think, for the soldiers spoke as if it was not on this road.

We arrived at Green River about three o'clock. The river is about as wide, deep and swift as the North Platte, yet I have not dreaded any of the rivers we have crossed as I did dread to ford this one. Perhaps it was because there are so few of us, for in numbers there is a feeling of security, even in crossing deep and dangerous streams. We crossed without accident or loss, and are camping on the west bank of Green River.

When we first came to the river, one of Mr. Curry's boys exclaimed:

"Well, this river is named right. If I had been going to name it, I believe I would have named it Green River, too, for it is green."

The water is very clear, yet the river has a bluish-green appearance. I do not understand why.

There are several corrals along the river, but the people are strangers, so we feel very much alone. There is a station here and soldiers' tents within sight. We are camping on blue grass, with the mountains very close. They are the highest I have seen. I would like to climb to the top, but mother says there are too many soldiers and strangers around.

At the foot of the mountain, a little way from our camp, there is a graveyard with about a dozen graves. It is a beautiful spot, with the mountain for an enduring monument. Several of the graves have been made this year, with names and dates quite distinct on the plain pine headboards. Others are entirely worn or washed off by the relentless hand of time and storm. It seems that Bitter Creek was too much for the weak or frail constitutions. Like Moses, they were permitted to look upon the better land before they died.

*　　*　　*　　*　　*

Monday, August 7.

The soldiers brought Hosstetter here in the night, and I suppose the witnesses came too. I wanted to go to the station to see if I could hear anything from Neelie, and the rest of the sick folks, but mother did not want me to go where there are so many soldiers, so I did not go. We started very early this morning and have driven about twenty miles. Are camping on Black Fork, where the horses and cattle are just wading in fine pasture right around camp.

We ascended a mountain this morning that was seven miles from base to summit, the way the road is. We had toilsome climbing, and I guess the teams found it a hard road to travel before we reached the top. I came on in advance of the wagons, sometimes riding and sometimes leading Dick where it was very steep, and had time to enjoy the magnificent scenery that lay spread out on all sides. The snowy range could be seen in the distance, glittering in the morning sunshine. The wild currants are here in abundance. I am going fishing with the boys, so I must be off.

WILD CURRANTS GALORE.

Tuesday, August 8.

We caught fish enough for breakfast last evening, and gathered currants enough for sauce, but I spoilt the sauce by putting the sugar in, when I put them on to cook, they hardened and were not fit to eat. I have been experimenting to-day and have succeeded in making a nice cobbler.

I did not sweeten at all before baking, but made the sauce sweet enough to sweeten all. I also made a fine sauce by cooking the currants only a very few minutes, and putting in the sugar after they were cooked. We will have currant dumplings for dinner to-morrow. We have picked a lot, enough to make sauce and pies and other good things for a week. The currants are a beautiful fruit, and some are as large as small cherries. We are waiting at Camp Plentiful, in the hope that some of the wagons from the train will drive in before night.

There are three wigwams within sight of our camp. Sim and Hillhouse went hunting to-day. On their way back they stopped at the wigwams and found them occupied by white men with squaws for wives. Ugh!

*　*　*　*　*

Wednesday, August 9.

Somehow I felt a little suspicious of those white men living with squaws, and feared some of our horses might be missing this morning, but my suspicions were groundless. Our horses and cattle were all here, well fed and ready for a long drive. We were off bright and early, without seeing any one from the train.

We passed the Bridger Road, where our friends going to California will turn off, so we are not likely to see them again, perhaps for years, perhaps never again in this life.

There is a very fine ranch at the junction of the roads, where we stopped at noon. Two men from this ranch visited our camp this evening. They were rather fine looking, genteel in appearance, dressed in civilization style, but for some unexplainable reason, I was afraid of them. They tried to be very cordial and polite. They engaged Sim in conversation, and plied him with pertinent questions, such as:

"Who owns those big American mares?" (referring to our horse team).

"They are the property of a widow."

"Whose bay pony is that?"

"It belongs to the widow's daughter."

"Who is the owner of that chestnut sorrel?"

"Mr. Curry, father of those boys playing over there."

They asked many more questions. Where we came from? Where we are going? What we expect to do, etc.

Sim answered them patiently and civilly. He thinks they are horse thieves, but hopes they will not be mean enough to steal from a widow. As if horse thieves care who they steal from. No doubt, their ranch is stocked with stolen horses and cattle, for they have things as they choose away out here, where there is no law, except the law of might.

God's Word says, "As the partridge sitteth on eggs, and hatcheth them not; so he that getteth riches, and not by right, shall leave them in the midst of his days, and at his end shall be a fool" (Jer. 17:11).

We are camping on Ham's Fork, where the currants and fish are very plentiful, and the pasture very fine. We had our currant dumplings for dinner. They were lovely. No one can imagine how we appreciate this fruit by the wayside, except those who have been deprived of the strawberries, raspberries, blackberries and cherries, each in their season, and confined to the sameness and tameness of diet, which people making this trip are necessarily confined to. This fruit would seem inferior among other cultivated fruits, but where it is, it seems a luxury provided for our benefit.

*　　*　　*　　*　　*

Thursday, August 10.

We went fishing at noon. It is such fun to fish in water so clear that we can see the fish biting at the hook. They do not seem at all afraid, and sometimes there will be two, three, or four grabbing at the hook at the same time. Such shoving, pushing and crowding as they all try to get the tempting bait. How eager and unsuspecting they are. Soon the strongest or fleetest, or rather the most unfortunate one seizes it. Away goes bait, hook and all, and then out comes a fish on dry land. I give a shiver of pity for the unlucky fish, as I call to the boys: "I have another."

It does seem such a cruel thing to take them from their pleasant home in the deep, clear, cool water. But then, "Life is sustained by death." And thousands upon thousands of lives are taken daily to nourish and sustain human life. We are in a beautiful place, where all things necessary for camping are plentiful, and we are all alone, no corral within sight; the first time we have been entirely alone.

*　　*　　*　　*　　*

Friday, August 11.

One or other of the boys stood guard last night. It proved an unnecessary precaution. There was no disturbance either from horse thieves, Indians, or wild beasts. We are living fine since we crossed Green River. We have fresh fish for breakfast and sometimes for dinner. Wild game of some kind for dinner, with currant pudding, cobbler, or dumplings, with rich

224

cream for dessert. We may possibly go hungry next Winter at Virginia City, but there is no danger of starving while we stay on Ham's Fork.

The weather is perfect. I have been riding my pony the greater part of the day, sometimes one of Mr. Curry's little boys with me, and sometimes alone. I have enjoyed the delightful atmosphere—it seems so pure and invigorating; the scenery is beautiful, and it has been a glorious day.

MR. CURRY'S HORSE STOLEN.

Saturday, August 12.

It was considered unnecessary for any one to stand guard last night, as we had come two days' travel from where the suspicious characters live. So all went to bed, retired early, slept soundly, and even neglected to put Cæsar's rug in its usual place—under our wagon—so he went into the tent with Mr. Curry's boys to find a comfortable bed, leaving the camp entirely unguarded. One of our big horses wears a bell. I was awakened in the night by hearing an unusual rattling, and the horses came galloping up to the wagons. Dick whinnied. I raised the wagon cover and spoke to him, and he commenced cropping the grass. The other horses were in sight, but not eating. They seemed frightened, and just then Cæsar came tearing out of the tent and ran toward the road barking fiercely. The moon was shining brightly. I looked out at the back of the wagon, but could not discover anything wrong, but evidently there was something wrong, for Mr. Curry's horse was gone this morning.

Mr. Curry, Sim and Hillhouse have been hunting the horse all day, but without success, except to find certain evidence that it had been stolen. They found the camp-fire, where three horses had been tied for some time. They then found where four horses had traveled, so they concluded there were three men after the horses.

The boys think it was the merest accident that our horses are not gone too, but I believe it was providential care that kept them for us. Mr. Curry is anxious to stay and try to recover his horse. I believe, as the boys do, that it will be a waste of effort, for if men are mean enough to steal a horse they will manage to keep it. But we do not like to offer too many objections, as it might seem like selfishness on our part, as we are not the losers.

Oh, dear, why don't people be good, and do as they would be done by? How much happier this world would be if there were no thieves nor wicked people in it. I know it is hard for Mr. Curry to give up his fine horse without making an effort to get it back. Yet I feel sure he will not get it. For if he found it he could not force the thieves to give it to him.

ANXIOUSLY WAITING AT HAM'S FORK.

Sunday, August 13.

It was decided this morning that Hillhouse, Sim and Mr. Curry would go in pursuit of the horse thieves. Sim is just recovering from a severe sickness, and is not able to go on such a trip, but he positively refused to stay in camp and let Hillhouse and Mr. Curry go without him. I believe it will prove a wild goose chase,

226

so mother and I exacted a promise from Hillhouse that he will not stay away to-night. We are looking for him. It is getting dark. Surely they will not leave us here in this wilderness with only two boys and Cæsar for protection. If we are left alone, I shall take my turn, with Winthrop and Alex Curry standing guard in camp. Sim rode Dick this morning, the others walked. What they expect to do if they find the thieves (which they are not likely to do) I do not know.

Mr. and Mrs. Kennedy, Mr. and Mrs. Bower, Nellie and Alton, and Mr. Grier's teams passed here to-day. They left the train the next morning after we did. The train had not started then. They said Neelie was about as when we left, and Mrs. Hardinbrooke was no worse.

*　　*　　*　　*　　*

Monday, August 14.

Hillhouse came in about an hour after dark. He was very tired and hungry; had walked since early morning until he started back at three o'clock. He tried to prevail upon Sim to return, and let him go on with Mr. Curry if he must go. But Sim would not listen to such a proposition, although he is still weak from his late sickness. Mr. Curry thinks he will find his horse at the ranch near the junction, although the trail they were following led away from, instead of toward it. If he finds it, he will go back to the train and get the men to help him get it either by fair means or by force.

He then proposed that they keep Dick, but they said he would not reach camp before midnight on foot and he might lose his way, but Dick would take him the shortest route if he would just let him go his own way, which he did, and he brought him safe about an hour after dark.

I am so sorry for Mrs. Curry. She tries to be brave for her children's sake, but any one can see she suffers, and Alex says she does not eat at all, just takes a cup of tea once in a while.

*　　*　　*　　*　　*

Tuesday, August 15.

Another day has come and gone, and the wanderers have not returned. Hillhouse said he did not expect them to-day, but would look for them to-morrow, for they will not have anything to eat after to-day, and will be obliged to leave the foot hills and come to the road, whether they find the horse or not, to get something to eat.

A party of emigrants stopped near us to-day at noon, and one of the men came to our camp. We, of course, asked if they had seen the Hardinbrooke train. They passed the train Sunday. They were still where we left them at the west end of Bitter Creek. He saw and talked to the captain, who told him to tell us, if he caught up with us, "The sick folks are all better, and they expect to come to Green River Monday." They may catch up with us yet.

I do not know what we would do with ourselves if it were not for the currants. We are making jelly, and as it takes lots of currants to make a little jelly, we have not suffered from enforced idleness, with our suspense and anxiety.

Wednesday, August 16.

There are three varieties of currants here. The yellow ones are not very plentiful. They are the largest and best. I have made a pickle jar full of the loveliest jelly. It is the color of gold and as clear as crystal. The red currants are very plentiful and more like the tame currants, though they do not yield as much juice.

We gather the bushes by the armful, and carry them to camp, and sitting near each other, we pick off the currants.

Though we do not talk much, we like to be near each other. Another day and they have not come, and another night of anxiety before us.

THE WANDERERS' RETURN.

Thursday, August 17.

I was awakened very early this morning, as soon as it was light, by hearing Hillhouse bustling about making a fire in the stove, as if in a hurry for his breakfast. I dressed as quickly as possible, and hastened out to see what it meant—for it was only four o'clock. When I asked for an explanation, he said:

"I am going to hunt those men. I can't stand this any longer. I have laid awake almost all night thinking about them."

"What can you do? You will be lost yourself."

"No danger of that. I will go back on the road as far as Green River, get some of the soldiers and some of the boys that know them, and we will hunt until we find them, or know what has become of them. I may meet them on the road and return to-night, but I will not come until I bring them with me, or know their fate."

I could not object to his going, but oh, how my heart sank at the thought.

We made all haste to get breakfast, and Hillhouse was all ready to start when Mrs. Curry and the boys came out. Mrs. Curry seemed both glad and sorry he was going, said she hardly knew which. I had supplied him with pencil and paper, and he promised to send us word every opportunity. He mounted Dick and rode away without saying good-bye.

He had gone almost out of sight. One moment more and a bend in the road would hide him from our view. When, lo, there is a gun fired not far off.

My thought was Indians, and I looked to see if Hillhouse was hurt. He was waving his hat furiously and came tearing back to camp. Then I heard Mrs. Curry cry out:

"Oh, it is my husband." And she dropped in a heap on the ground, and cried out loud.

They were plainly visible by that time, coming over the hill and down to the creek and through it, before any one could show them where they could cross without getting wet.

All was excitement for a while. The meeting between Mr. Curry and his family was very touching, indeed. I think Mrs. Curry had about lost all hope of ever seeing him again.

How famished and worn out they did seem to be. Sim was utterly exhausted. I do not believe he could have gone another half mile. We gave Sim a bowl of bread and milk, and a cup of coffee. Then the boys helped him to bed in our wagon, because it is on springs and we expected to start before he waked. Within one hour after they reached camp Sim was sleeping the sleep of exhaustion. We did not ask any questions, nor let him talk at all, before he went to sleep.

Mrs. Curry prepared the best breakfast the camp could afford for her husband, and as the family had not breakfasted, they all sat down together. She came for Sim to take breakfast with them, but he was sound asleep, and I would not have had him awakened for the best breakfast ever prepared. Perhaps Mr. Curry can stand eating such a meal after starving so long, but I believe it would kill Sim in his weak condition, for he is not fully recovered from his recent illness.

We made all haste to start once more, and by eight o'clock were on the way. We had left the camp where we spent five such anxious, distressful days. Sim did not awaken until after ten o'clock. We gave him some fish and bread and milk, which we had ready for him. When he had eaten, he lay in bed and told mother and I the following narrative of what had befallen them since they left camp:

SIM'S STORY OF THEIR WANDERINGS.

"After Hill left us that first afternoon, we walked on as fast as we could, as long as we could follow the trail. Then made a fire, ate some supper without anything to drink. We had not seen water since noon.

"We rolled up in our blankets and lay down with our feet to the fire and tried to sleep. I am sure I did not sleep an hour, I was so tired and nervous. As soon as it was light enough to see, we were up and ate a dry breakfast, for we could find no water in the vicinity. We were soon following the trail. Before night we had eaten all our grub, and found no water. Oh, what would I have given for a cup of cold water? It seemed that we must find water or perish. We dragged on as long as we could see; then lay down and slept from exhaustion. When we awoke it was light.

"I was so weak that Mr. Curry had to help me to get on my feet. I declared I could go no further. Mr. Curry prevailed on me to try, for we must be near Green River. I made a desperate effort, and dragged on for half a mile perhaps, Mr. Curry carrying my blanket, when I positively could go no further, and told Mr. Curry to go on and leave me and try to save himself. Mr. Curry was desperate. He said: 'I must find something to eat.' He covered me with the blankets and went to look for some kind of game.

"When he had gone about a hundred yards he saw a bird about the size of a partridge sitting on a limb ready to be shot. He took careful aim and shot its head off. He hastened back to where I lay, made a fire, skinned the bird, and held it on a sharpened stick before the fire and roasted it thoroughly. I would have eaten it when half done, but Mr. Curry would not let me have it until well cooked, for fear it would make me sick.

"I never tasted fowl that tasted so good as that did, although we ate it without salt. After eating I felt better, and made another effort to move on. We had gone only a little way when Mr. Curry stopped, listened a moment, and exclaimed: 'There, hear the rushing of the river?'

"I could not hear it at first, but soon I heard the glad sound too. It gave us courage, and with renewed energy we pushed on, and before eleven o'clock we reached the river. We slacked our thirst, cautiously, at first, then had a bath and were refreshed.

"While I rested on the bank, Mr. Curry looked up and down the river for the trail, which had gone into the river. He did not find it. We then started for the road, which we came into in about an hour, just below the ranch at the junction.

"A party of emigrants had stopped for noon, who gladly gave food and refreshment to us weary wanderers. While I was resting, Mr. Curry investigated the ranch, looked among the horses in the pasture, peeped in stables, but did not find his horse.[2]

"After Mr. Curry had given up getting his horse he was all eagerness to get back to his family, but considering how very weak I was, he consented to stay with the kind people we had fallen in with until morning, so we traveled with them, and I rested in a wagon all afternoon.

"At the first peep of dawn Mr. Curry was up and awakened me. I felt refreshed and ready for our early walk. Mr. Curry explored the grub-box, found some

---

[2] Those men at the junction did steal Mr. Curry's horse. The men in the Hardinbrooke train saw them in their corral, and asked, "Where did you get that horse?" They answered, "From a man by the name of Curry. Paid $150 for him."

bread and meat, which he appropriated, leaving green-backs to pay for our entertainment.

"We expected to reach camp by ten o'clock P. M., but I gave completely out, and we were obliged to lie down and rest when about five miles from camp. I slept until awakened this morning before it was light by Mr. Curry, who was so anxious to be on the way I wondered that he let me sleep so long.

"We came over the foot-hills, instead of by the road, and saved about a mile in distance. We saw Hill riding away from camp and felt sure he was starting to try and find us. Mr. Curry fired his gun to attract his attention, and you know the rest."

He turned over and went to sleep again, and slept until we stopped for noon. We made a long drive to-day and are camping at the foot of Bear River mountain.

We had a hard rain and hail storm this afternoon. It was very violent while it lasted, and we halted by the roadside until it was over. It was over in half an hour.

Mr. Curry has suffered with a severe headache and high fever all day, the result of that hearty breakfast this morning after fasting so long.

BEAR RIVER MOUNTAIN.

Friday, at noon, August 18.

I am on the summit of Bear River Mountain, in the border of a beautiful grove of pine and quaking-asp, near a spring of the most delicious ice-cold water. I must be some miles ahead of the wagons that I left toiling up the steep mountain side. Yet I do not feel that

I am alone. Oh, no. I feel that God is here in his might, majesty, power and glory. I feel His nearness now, and as I gaze from these dizzy heights upon the country spread out beneath my feet, I am lost in admiration, the scene is so grand, so magnificent, that I forget my own vanity and nothingness. I feel that I am standing upon an altar raised by Nature's grateful hand up to Nature's God, and that I could offer myself a willing sacrifice.

This is emphatically one of the high and sacred spots of earth. How manifold, how wonderful are the works of Nature: Everywhere something worthy of our highest admiration is presented to view; everywhere do we see the manifestation of an invisible and omnipotent Creator. The terrific storm, the broad prairies, the majestic forest, excite within our bosoms emotions of awe and admiration, yet there are no places on earth that I have seen which have a tendency to inspire me with such tender feelings, such elevated, pure, holy thoughts as mountains.

Oh, it seems that one could never sin, or have an evil thought, in such a place as this. Behold the mountains as they stand upon their broad bases, contemplate them as they rear their snowy tops in awful, majestic grandeur above the clouds, view them as you will, and they ever present the same untiring pleasure to the mind.

Men and women will travel thousands of miles and make the greatest exertion to climb the rugged steeps of mountains, to enjoy for one short hour the charming prospect. I have wondered at this sometimes, as I have read of their hazardous exploits in trying to obtain a point where they could have the finest view, but I never shall again.

A country destitute of mountains may be fertile and productive of all that conduces to human happiness, yet it will lack the essential of attractive moral grandeur.

It may enchant the imagination for a moment to look over prairies and plains as far as the eye can reach, still such a view is tedious and monotonous. It can in no wise produce that rapturing delight, that pleasing variety of the sublime and beautiful of landscape scenery which mountains afford.

Let those whose tastes are on a level with the ground they tread feel proud of and admire their prairie fields, but give to me a mountain home.

The wagons are almost at the top, and as mother has driven up the steep ascent, I will drive down the western slope, and have mother ride Dick, and enjoy the delightsome scenery as we descend the mountain-side, which looks very steep from here.

We were all the evening crossing the mountain, and it was a hard drive. We are camping at the foot of the mountain near a spring in Bear River Valley, within calling distance of the Chilicothe train.

We passed two freight wagons on the mountain-side that were rather badly smashed up. One had upset, and crackers in a broken-up condition, and other debris from family groceries were scattered about.

We learned that the wagons are Dr. Yager's, and he has gone somewhere to get the wheels mended. We are quite disappointed that he is away, for Sim is not so well as he was yesterday, has had fever and been flighty and in a stupor this afternoon. He needs medical treatment, and we hoped to have Dr. Yager prescribe for him.

We passed eight graves on the mountain, one a young lady twenty years old from Monroe County, Missouri. A beautiful resting place for the dead. Mrs. Yager is quite sick, and seems sadly disheartened. Thinks crossing the plains and mountains in a wagon (they have a very comfortable carriage) is a sad, discouraging, never-to-be-repeated experiment. I am sorry she could not enjoy the fine prospect on the mountain-top, for she is a lady who would appreciate such grandeur to the fullest under favorable circumstances.

We reached level ground without accident, and were glad to come up with friends we had met before on the road.

WE MEET CAPTAIN HARDINBROOKE'S BROTHER.

Saturday, August 19.

We left the Chilicothe train this morning. As it will take all day to get the wagons mended, they cannot start to-day. We came on to Bear River, reached here a little after noon, and will stay here until to-morrow.

We crossed a toll bridge on Smith's Fork, and met Captain Hardinbrooke's brother at the bridge. He is going to meet the train. He did not know of Mrs. Hardinbrooke's illness. He asked very especially and with some confusion, "Is Miss Walker well?"

Ah, I think I know who he is going to meet, and understand some things that have not been very clear to me before. "Ah, ha, Miss Lyde, you have guarded your secret well, but see if I have not guessed it now?" Well, he is very nice looking, and if he makes as good a husband as his brother, he will no doubt be worth coming to Montana for. I wish you joy, and that I may be present at the wedding festivities.

The boys have gone fishing, all but Sim. Poor boy he is too sick again. I feel very much out of patience with Mr. Curry, because of the tramp he led Sim when in so weak a condition.

*   *   *   *   *

Sunday, August 20.

We passed a grave this morning that was made yesterday for a young mother and her new-born babe. Oh, how sad. With what an aching heart must that husband and father go on his weary way, leaving his loved ones by the roadside.

We crossed another toll bridge. It seems to me that emigrants are greatly imposed upon by these men who claim toll. They throw a very poor excuse of a bridge across a stream that could be easily forded if let alone, but they spoil the crossing by digging ditches and throwing in bush and timbers to obstruct the fording, then build a cabin, close to the bridge, and squat to make a fortune by extorting large toll from emigrants, who have not the time to stop and contend for their rights. It seems a shameful business.

While stopping at noon we saw a company of Indians coming down the road toward our wagons. My first sensation was fear, but upon reflection I knew that is not the way they go on the warpath, and by the time they reached camp I was ready to say "How," and try to talk to them. There was one that could understand English and talked quite well.

They are Bannocks, the tribe that was conquered in Idaho some years ago. Their chief was with them. He held a stiff neck and tried to look dignified, and only looked ridiculous. They are going on a buffalo hunt. It seems that the whole tribe are going, squaws, pappooses and all.

We have been meeting them all afternoon and are camping with them all around us to-night. They all seem to want my pony. I have been asked at least twenty times this afternoon to "Swap." I gave all the same answer, "No swap." Why, I would not give my Dick for twenty of their ponies.

The squaws and pappooses are around our camp to-night begging biscuit. They are the greatest beggars I ever saw. I do wonder if they are hungry?

We crossed the steepest, straight up and down mountain to-day that we have crossed yet. It seemed that the wagons would turn a somersault as we were making the descent.

Sim was too sick to sit up, and he would slide down in a heap, bed, bedclothes and all, against the seat and grub-box. We stopped twice to have him helped back into place. When we reached level ground he was all piled up again. Poor Sim, he is very sick. I do wish we could come across a physician. We have administered simple remedies, but seemingly without effect.

There is an old lady ninety-three years old in a train camping near us to-night. She is cheerful as a lark, sings sometimes, and is an incessant talker.

She says she is going to Oregon, where she expects to renew her youth. She looks very old and wrinkled in the face, but is very active in her movements, and not at all stooped. The people she is with are not at all refined or cultured, but I do like to talk to the old lady, she is so quaint. It makes mother seem quite a young woman to see her with an old lady more than forty years older than she is. Why, she seems just in the prime of life, and we had thought her growing old.

MORMON TOWNS IN IDAHO.

Monday, August 21.

Since we crossed the last steep mountain the horse flies have been very troublesome, the first that have bothered us all summer. I wonder if the Indians brought them?

We came through two villages to-day; they are about five miles apart. The first Bennington, the last Montpelier—pretty large names for such small places. They are Mormon towns, although this is Idaho Territory. The women appeared sad and sorrowful enough to be the wives of Mormons. I did not see one of them smile. Our wagons were thronged with women and children selling butter, eggs, cheese and vegetables. They sold eggs at seventy-five cents per dozen, butter seventy cents per pound, cheese fifty cents, potatoes twenty-five cents, and everything else in proportion. The prices seemed enormous to us, but I presume we would have purchased if they had been double what they were, for we are about starved for such things. Just think of spending a whole summer without garden productions.

This is a beautiful valley. Too good to be possessed by a community of bigamists. What a stigma upon the Government of these United States that whole communities are allowed to live criminal lives with impunity. I wonder how many are paying the penalty for bigamy in the penitentiaries of the United States? What is crime in one place, under the same Government, I would think, would be crime in all other places, if the one did happen to be an isolated case, while the other is in large numbers, or wholesale. I suppose I am not well enough versed in law and politics to understand why it is crime in one place and not in the other. We are camping eight miles from Montpelier. Sim is much better to-day.

*   *   *   *   *

Tuesday, August 22.

Here we are at Soda Springs. I am surprised to see so small a town, for it is quite an old place for this western country, at least ten or fifteen years old, and does not have a post-office. The town is beautifully situated, the landscape views are glorious. The soda springs are bubbling up out of the ground in many places in this vicinity, and I expect there will be a city here some day. There are medicinal springs here that possess wonderful curative properties, or people think they do. We wanted Sim to test them, but he said:

"I am getting well as fast as possible, and I don't care to drink that nauseous water. I prefer the pure, unadulterated snow water from the mountain springs."

This is the junction of the Oregon and Montana roads. There are three camps within sight of us.

Wednesday, August 23.

As we drove into the road this morning there was a train of eight wagons came into line just behind our wagons, and have traveled with us all day, stopping at noon when we did, and they are camping near us to-night, though we have separate camps. They are from Missouri, and are going to Virginia City. They seem to think as we all came from the same State, and our destination is the same place, that of course there is a bond of fellowship that is mutual, but to be frank, I must confess I do not care to go into a strange place in their company, for I fear we would be judged by the company we keep, and I think it would not be very favorable, so we will try to get away from them as soon as possible.

The weather is perfect. This is a beautiful valley. The men say the land is extremely rich. We are camping on the Blackfoot. We have not been able to shake our Missouri friends.

WE MEET MEN RETURNING TO THE STATES.

Thursday, August 24.

We came to a toll bridge over the Blackfoot this morning, where the toll was one dollar per team, and fifty cents for horseback riders. There had been an excellent ford just below the bridge. The men collecting the toll had spoiled it by digging ditches on both sides near the bank. The water was clear, and they were plainly visible. Hillhouse mounted Dick to see if we could ford it. One of the men screamed out at him: "You will mire your horse if you try that."

242

"I'll risk it." And he rode in below where the ditches were dug. The pony's feet were not muddy. Hillhouse found we could easily ford the creek below the ditches, which we did without accident.

It does seem a shame that we should have to pay toll for crossing a stream like that, after fording South Platte, North Platte and Green River.

The Missourians refused to pay the exorbitant price, and offered them fifty cents per wagon. They swore they would not take a cent less than one dollar. But the travelers were too many for them, and they drove over and did not pay a cent. The toll men were fearfully angry, and made great threats, but the men dared them to do their worst and laughed at them.

I do hope we will get ahead of these people to-morrow. They are not the kind of people I like to travel with.

We have met as many as twenty men to-day going back to the States from the Virginia City mines. George Mays was with them. I mentioned about his leaving the train to go through on horseback, expecting to get his meals at stations and emigrant trains, when his brother with his bride went to Colorado. Says he worked just one day and got five dollars for it, and took the back track the next day.

"Mining is the only work a man can get to do, and it would kill an ordinary man in less than a week."

He is distressingly homesick. He is going to Denver to his brother.

*   *   *   *   *

243

We were up at the first peep of dawn, had breakfast, and were hitching up to start, when the folks in the eight wagons began to emerge and light their camp fires, so we have left them some distance behind. We have been meeting men all day returning from the mines. They give a doleful account of the hard times in Montana. They say: "There are a few fortunate ones who are making money like dirt, but they are the exception, about one in a hundred."

One man was very anxious to buy Dick. I told him: "This pony is not for sale," and rode away before he could say anything more. The boys say we have met as many as two hundred men to-day returning from the mines. I believe we are all somewhat discouraged this evening. We have always heard such flattering reports from Alder Gulch and Virginia City.

*   *   *   *   *

Friday, August 26.

We have overtaken Mr. Grier, Mr. Bower and Mr. Kennedy. Some of Mr. Bower's cattle have eaten a poisonous herb—wild larkspur, I believe it is. One ox has died and several are poisoned, but will not die. They got the poison weed the day before yesterday, when they stopped at noon. I am glad we have overtaken them, but sorry for their misfortune. Hillhouse has just now come in, and says Joe, one of our big white oxen, is poisoned. He came for remedies and to sharpen his knife to bleed him. No doubt he got the poison the same place Mr. Bower's cattle did when we stopped for noon. Sim, Hillhouse and Winthrop have gone to his relief.

MOTHER AND I SAVE JOE'S LIFE.

Later.—The boys came back very much discouraged after working an hour, and said: "The blood will not flow, and he is swelling frightfully. I fear he will die, for when the blood will not run and the animal begins to swell, they cannot be saved."

Mother said: "We will not let him die without further effort, at least. Come on, Sarah, let us try what we can do for him."

We melted a quart of lard and put it in a long-necked bottle (that we had brought for the purpose of drenching horses or cattle), cut up a lot of fat bacon into strips, put on our big aprons, and taking a bucket of cold water, we were ready. Hillhouse said: "Don't give him water." I answered, "You never mind, who is doing this?"

We were not long finding poor Joe. He seemed to be suffering dreadfully. His nose was as hot as fire. It actually burned my hands when I took hold of it to drench him with the lard. He seemed to know we were trying to help him, and did not resist at all when I put the bottle in the side of his mouth to pour the lard down his throat. He looked at us with his great, soft, patient eyes in such a docile, knowing manner, I felt sure he would not bite me, so I put my hand away down his throat to make him swallow the strips of fat bacon. He swallowed them as patiently as if he knew what they were for. We then bathed his nose with the cold water, without letting him drink any, and before we came away he seemed relieved, and the swelling had stopped and he breathed much better. I believe he will live.

*   *   *   *   *

Saturday, August 27.

Joe did not die. This morning when Hillhouse went to see about him, expecting to find him dead, he was grazing, and seemed as well as ever, except his nose, which looks as if it had been scalded.

We came to Snake River ferry this morning, six miles from where we camped last night. We paid eight dollars for our outfit crossing on the ferry. As Nellie Bower and I were standing on the bank of the river watching the wagons being ferried over, holding our ponies by their bridles, a gentleman came near. Lifting his hat and bowing politely, he said to me: "I will give one hundred dollars in clean gold dust for that pony." "This pony is not for sale, sir, at any price."

We came from the ferry about two miles, and stopped for lunch. I told Hillhouse what the man said.

"If I were you, I would certainly sell him, so many seem to want him. He will very likely be stolen."

"Oh, I can't sell my pony."

After lunch the men folks went to fish in Snake River. They had been gone but a few minutes, when the man that wanted Dick rode into camp. He rode straight to our wagons, and said:

"I will give you one hundred and ten dollars for that pony."

I had begun to relent somewhat. I felt that it would not do to be sentimental under existing circumstances. We had spent almost all our money for toll, ferrying and other expenses on the road. It might prove to be a serious matter to be in a strange place without money, and if we fail to get employment we will be obliged to sell something, and there is nothing we can spare so well as Dick. I knew the man had offered all and more than I could expect to get for him.

But as Hillhouse was gone fishing and I could not think of selling my pony myself, I said to the man:

"My brother is not here, and I cannot let him go."

"Tell your brother to bring him to the ferry, and I will send you the pay for him."

"I think you need not expect him, for I am sure he will not come."

He went away without Dick, and Hillhouse did not take him back, so I have my pony yet. We came five miles and camped, as too long a drive is not good for the poisoned cattle. I wish there was a longer distance between us and the man that wants my pony.

Mr. Grier sold his riding horse at the ferry. He says:

"There is a party of half a dozen gentlemen going to the States horseback. They are all supplied, except the man that wants your pony. He has waited, trying to find a horse with an easy gait, and Dick is the only one that has suited him. Oh, he will be back again, Miss Raymond, and make another offer, and if you do not let him have him, I don't know what he will do, for he seems determined to get him."

If he does come I will not dare to refuse him, but I do hope we are out of reach of temptation. Dick is as fat as when we started. I comb and brush him every day, and he shows his keeping. He always looks nice and sleek. He is a bright bay, with heavy black mane and tail.

DICK IS SOLD. OH, DEAR.

Sunday, August 28.

It was scarcely daylight when that hateful man was here again after Dick. I had just finished dressing when Hillhouse came to the wagon and said:

"Shall I let Dick go?"

"Do as you think best." And I threw myself on the bed for a good cry. I had not stopped crying when he came back, and throwing a buckskin purse into my lap, said:

"There is your pony." There was one hundred and twenty-five dollars in gold dust in it. I sobbed out loud. Hillhouse looked at me with contempt in his expression, but said nothing. I could not help crying.

I know he would never sell anything that he loved, and I love that pony. I let the purse roll out of my lap down into the bottom of the wagon, and have not touched it yet. Of course, I knew the wagon-bed was tight, and there is no danger of its being lost. We came to Silver Lake to-day. We are having a fine shower of rain, which we were needing very much. It was some time coming, so we had dinner over and were ready for it when it reached us.

Monday, August 29.

We have traveled to-day over Snake River desert, nothing but sand and sage-brush. We watered at noon at a toll well, called Hole-in-the-sand, and paid ten cents a head for watering stock. I wonder what we will have to pay toll for next?

We are camping on Camel's Creek. There is a family camping near us from Bannack, going to the States. The lady is a sister of Mr. Esler, one of the quartz kings of Montana, so she says; I presume everybody knows about him, but I must confess I never heard of him until now.

His sister is taking his motherless babe back to its grandmother. Mr. Esler's wife died more than a month ago. The babe is about four months old, and as sweet as can be. I could not keep my hands off it, and that is how I came to get acquainted with its auntie. She is a great talker, seems to think I am going to Montana husband-hunting, and volunteered a deal of advice on the subject, especially I must not tell that I am from Missouri, as Missourians are below par in Montana. She is from New York. Oh, dear, it makes one tired to see a full-grown woman so frivolous.

*　　　*　　　*　　　*　　　*

Tuesday, August 30.

We watered the stock at noon at Hole-in-the-rock. Didn't turn them out to graze, as there was nothing for them to graze on.

Mr. Bower has lost another ox, and was obliged to buy a yoke of oxen to get his wagons over the ranges. There are two mountains to cross before he reaches his home in the Madison Valley, fifteen or twenty miles the other side of Virginia City. Of course, he had to pay a most exorbitant price. Joe, our ox that was poisoned, seems as well as ever, except his nose has peeled off as if scalded into a blister.

We are camping at the foot of the last range we will cross before we reach our destination.

Mrs. Kennedy and I have become quite well acquainted the last few days. She was a bride of only a few days when they started to the West. Her husband drives one of Mr. Bower's teams. They are going among strangers, to make them a home and fortune. She is a very intelligent and well-educated young woman. I do not know her husband very much.

MOTHER'S BIRTHDAY.

Wednesday, August 31.

Mother's birthday. She is fifty-three years old. We have not been able to celebrate it especially, yet she is not likely to forget it, though spent in climbing a Rocky Mountain range. We have been now four months on this journey. Have lived out of doors, in all sorts of weather. It has been very beneficial to mother. She was looking frail and delicate when we started, but seems to be in perfect health now, and looks at least ten years younger.

I have not heard her utter one word of complaint, either of physical suffering or outward discomfort, such as the heat or cold, mud, dust, rain, nor any of the things that make camping out disagreeable, and so many people grumble about. "What can't be cured, must be endured," is her motto, and the one care has been that we all keep in good health, and she would ask nothing more.

We are camping in Pleasant Valley, a depression right on top of the mountain, just large enough for a good-sized ranch. It is a beautiful place, the scenery is magnificently grand. There is a fine grove of beautiful trees at the lower end of the vale. The sides and upper end are hedged in by straight up and down hills or mountain-sides, about fifteen feet high. The grass is a luxuriant green and very plentiful.

There is a station here, occupied by a family that used to live in Virginia City. They have two very bright little girls, who have spent the early evening hours with us. They are perfect little chatterboxes to talk. They have a married sister living in Virginia City, the wife of a Mr. Wheeler, who is a candidate for some office. The little girls had forgotten whether for sheriff or Member of Congress.

*　　　*　　　*　　　*　　　*

Thursday, September 1.

This is brother Mac's birthday. He is twenty-seven years old. I wonder if he has thought of it, and remembered us. I presume he has. It has been some weeks since we have had an opportunity to post a letter to him. There have been depredations by the Indians, which have no doubt been largely reported in the newspapers, and he cannot know that we have escaped. His anxiety and suspense must be hard to

251

bear. I know I should suffer agonies were our circumstances reversed.

As we were descending the mountain we met a freight train loaded with people returning to the States. After we had passed them about half a mile, Hillhouse was walking in front of the wagons, and found a miner's shovel. It is bright and shining, but not new. It is worn off some. The men tell Hillhouse it is a good omen, that he will make money by the shovelful. He laughed, and said: "I reckon I'd better keep it, then, to shovel it up with."

*　　*　　*　　*　　*

Friday, September 2.

When I awoke in the night I heard the rain pattering on the wagon-cover. This morning the mountains were all covered with snow, and presented a magnificent picture. Those nearest our camp are covered with pine trees of an intensely dark green. The snow on the boughs and beneath the trees glittered in the sunshine. The scene was constantly changing, as the warm sun melted the snow from the boughs, and before night it was all gone except on the highest peaks, where it stays all summer.

The roads have been sloppy and muddy to-day, though the water has all run off or evaporated, so that it is comparatively dry where we are camping, notwithstanding there was so much snow and water on the ground this morning. It is too cold for comfort this evening. We are hovering around the stove with our shawls on.

SWEET WATER CAÑON.

Saturday, September 3.

We came through a deep, dark cañon this morning, and passed the grave of a man that was robbed and murdered last week. It is the deepest and darkest cañon we have traveled through. Ten men have been robbed and murdered in it in the last two years. We were in no danger of being molested. Only men who have their fortunes in gold about their person are intercepted, robbed and killed. How awful it seems. Why will men be so wicked?

In several places in the cañon the road has been widened with pick and shovel, perhaps two or three days' work done, and we had to pay ten dollars toll for our two wagons passing over it. We stopped at noon on Black Tail Deer Creek. Are camping on the Sweet Water, about twenty-five miles from Virginia City. This is a beautiful place. There are fine large trees along the creek, high mountains around a lovely dale. It is just large enough for a fine farm. There is a deserted cabin here, where some one commenced improving a farm, became homesick and discouraged, and left it for some one else.

*   *   *   *   *

Sunday, September 4.

We are camping within seven miles of Virginia City, near a freight train of about fifty wagons, with from seventy-five to one hundred people all together, men, women and children, returning to the States.

To hear these people talk of the disadvantages and disagreeable things with regard to life in Montana, would have a tendency to discourage one, if it were not so palpable that they are homesick, and everyone knows that when that disease is fairly developed, everything is colored with a deep dark blue, and even pleasant things seem extremely disagreeable to the afflicted person. The ladies seem to have the disease in its worst form, and of course they make the gentlemen do as they wish, which is to take them home to mother and other dear ones.

We have had a very pleasant day, about as pleasant as the day we started on this journey, the first day of May. It is cheering that the first and last days of our journeying should be so lovely. After four months and four days of living outdoors we are all in the most robust health. Yet we shall be glad to have a roof over our heads once more, even if it is a dirt roof.

*   *   *   *   *

Monday, September 5.

Noon.—Here we are camping in the suburbs of the city, in Alder Gulch, where the miners are at work. How I wish my descriptive powers were adequate to making those who have never seen gulch-mining see as I see, and realize the impression made upon me as I first looked into the gulch at the miners at work. There is a temporary bridge (very shaky) across the gulch that wagons may pass over. Standing on this bridge, in the middle of the gulch, looking up and down, and even beneath my feet, the scene is a lively one. So many men, it seems they would be in each other's way. They remind one of bees around a hive. And such active work. It seemed that not one of that great multitude stopped for one instant shoveling and wheeling dirt, passing and repassing each other without a hitch. It made me tired to look at them. The ground is literally turned inside out; great deep holes and high heaps of dirt. The mines are said to be very rich.

2 P. M.—We dined at noon to-day. Had beefsteak at fifty cents per pound and potatoes at twenty-five cents. I do not know if the price had anything to do with it, but it certainly tasted better than any I ever ate before.

I interviewed a woman—or rather she interviewed me—that lives near where we are camping. She said her name is Neihart. Her husband is a miner and earns seven dollars per day. Judging from the manner in which they seem to live, they ought to save at least five of it. I presume I did not make a very favorable impression, for after I came back to camp she called across the street to her neighbor—so we could hear what she said:

"Some more aristocrats. They didn't come here to work. Going to teach school and play lady," with great contempt in her voice.

I laughed at the first impression made, and tried to realize that teaching is not work.

THE END OF OUR JOURNEY.

Mrs. Curry, Sim, Hillhouse and I are going to town as soon as Mrs. Curry is ready. We held a council whether we should get out our street suits and last summer's hats, or go in our emigrant outfits, sun-bonnets and short dresses, thick shoes and all. Decided in favor of the latter. No doubt the people of Virginia are used to seeing emigrants in emigrant outfits, and we will not astonish them.

Evening.—We were not very favorably impressed with Virginia City. It is the shabbiest town I ever saw, not a really good house in it. Hillhouse and I, after hunting up and down the two most respectable looking streets, found a log cabin with two rooms that we rented for eight dollars per month. Mrs. Curry did not find a house at all. We thought as so many were leaving there would be an abundance of vacant houses, but there were enough living in tents to fill all the houses that were vacated.

Mr. Curry's folks and Mr. Kennedy's will go to Helena. Mr. Bower has a ranch on the Madison Valley. Mr. Grier will stay here for a time, anyway.

The cabin is on the corner of Wallace and Hamilton Streets, next door to the city butcher. The cabin has a dirt roof. There is a floor in it, and that is better than some have. It is neat and clean, which is a comfort. Men have not bached in it.

We found quite a budget of letters at the post-office, the most important of which are from brother Mac and Frank Kerfoot. Mac's letter:

CINCINNATI, August 10, 1865.

Dear Mother, Sister and Brothers:

It is with fear and trembling that I pen this letter. I have not heard from you for more than a month, telling me you had decided to go to Montana. The papers are full of accounts of Indian depredations. I have realized to the fullest extent that "Hope deferred maketh the heart sick." In your last letter you had decided to go to Virginia City, so I will direct this letter to be held until called for. I am glad you are not going any farther West. I cannot conceive why you wanted to go to that far off wild Western country. I do wish you had stopped at Omaha, or St. Jo, or even Denver. It would have been better than Montana. With sincerest love to all,

Your son and brother,
MAC.

But oh, the sad, sad news comes in Frank's letter. Neelie is dead. Oh, the anguish of soul, the desolateness of heart that one sentence gives expression to. Frank's letter:

GREEN RIVER, Wyoming Ter., Aug. 18

Dear Miss Sallie—

I write to tell you of our very great sorrow. Precious Neelie is gone. We are all sorely bereaved, but how Uncle Ezra's family can ever get along without her, I cannot see. Any member of the family, except uncle, could be spared better than Neelie. She got very much better, and the doctor said if uncle would stay there another week, he was sure Neelie would be well enough to travel without danger of a relapse, but if she had another relapse she could not be saved.

The Hardinbrooke train left Monday morning. Mrs. Hardinbrooke was much better. The Gatewoods and Ryans stayed with us. Neelie was much better. She sat up in bed some. That night Uncle Ezra did not sleep

257

at all, he was so afraid of Indians. The next morning, as Neelie had a good night's rest, and was feeling stronger, nothing else would do but we must move on to Green River, where the soldiers are. We started about nine o'clock, and drove twenty-five miles without stopping. It was very hot and dusty. Uncle drove the family wagon and watched Neelie carefully. After a time she seemed to be sleeping quietly, so he thought she was all right. But it was the sleep from which there is no waking in this life.

Dr. Howard and Dr. Fletcher were both at Green River, and they both worked all night trying to arouse her, but without success. At early dawn Neelie's sweet spirit took its flight, and we are left desolate.

Miss Sallie, do you remember Carpenter? the young man that made Uncle Ezra so mad by pretending to go into hysterics when the Ryan girls were leaving the train? When he heard that Neelie was gone, he went out on the mountain and found a large, smooth, flat stone, white as marble, but not so hard, and engraved Neelie's name, age, and date of her death on it, to mark her resting place. He worked all day upon it, and at the funeral he placed it at the head of her grave, and if you ever go over this road it will not be hard to find Neelie's grave. We gathered wild flowers and literally covered her grave with them.

Darling Neelie, our loss is her gain, for we all know that she was an earnest, devoted Christian. We will start on our now sorrowful journey to-morrow. I wish you were here to go with us, but hope you will be successful where you are, and happy too.

Mrs. Hardinbrooke was much worse after they came here. That hot, dusty drive was hard on well people; for sick people it was terrible. When Neelie died she was very low, but she has rallied, and the rest of the train will move on to-morrow. But Mr. Hardinbrooke will stay here with his wife until she is entirely restored, and they will go to Virginia City on the coach. All send love to you all. Aunt Mildred asked me to write you.

Very sincerely your friend,
FRANK.

I believe I am homesick this evening. It is so dreary to go into a strange place and meet so many people, and not one familiar face. But I must not complain, for we are all here, not even Cæsar missing. My heart aches so for the Kerfoots. I do not know how they can bear this terrible bereavement under such trying circumstances.

* * * * *

Tuesday, September 6.

Mr. Curry's folks have started to Helena. Mr. Bower's to the Madison Valley, and Mr. Kennedy with them, to drive his team, leaving Mrs. Kennedy with us until to-morrow, when they will take the coach for Helena.

We moved into our cabin this morning. It does not seem as much like home as the wagons did, and I believe we are all homesick if we would acknowledge it.

The boys found a checkerboard nailed on the window where a pane of glass was broken out. We pasted paper over the place. They made checkermen out of pasteboard, and Sim and Winthrop are having a game. Hillhouse is reading the Montana Post. Mother is making bread, and initiating Mrs. Kennedy into the mysteries of yeast and bread-making.

As Hillhouse was on his way to the butcher shop, he passed an auction sale of household goods. The auctioneer was crying a beautiful porcelain lamp. He stopped to make the first bid. "One dollar" he called. There were no other bids and he got the lamp—his first purchase in Virginia City. (He has it yet.)

When he brought it home, with the meat he went to get, mother said: "What is the use of the lamp without the chimney?"

So he went to purchase a chimney after dinner and coal oil to burn in the lamp. He had to pay two dollars and fifty cents for a chimney, and five dollars for a gallon of coal oil, so our light is rather expensive after all. And thus ends our first day in Virginia City, and brings "Crossing the Plains and Mountains in 1865" to an end.

By S. R. H.

Endnote

The Raymond family arrived in Virginia City by wagon train from Missouri in September 1865. They were Mrs. Delilah Raymond and her children Sarah (Sallie), William Hillhouse, and Winthrop. Mrs. Raymond started a boarding house and the boys soon had purchased a ranch they called Belmont Park .

Sarah began teaching school in March, 1866 as probably the first public school teacher in an organized school district in the Montana Territory. After teaching for one school year, Sarah married James M. Herndon in May 1867 and remained in Virginia City until her death in 1914. Sarah had kept a diary of the wagon train trip which was published in 1902 as "Days on the Road." She also kept a 1866 diary of her experiences in Virginia City and teaching school.

The Raymond family was prominent in Virginia City and Madison County. They began a successful freight company and the Raymond Brothers store. W. Hillhouse took over Belmont Park which became renowned for its trotters and Winthrop platted the town of Sheridan, Montana where he was in banking and land development. Mrs. Raymond died in 1896, W. Hillhouse in 1905 and Winthrop in 1912.[3]

---

[3] From the guide to the Sarah Raymond Herndon Papers, 1866-1912, (Montana State University-Bozeman Library, Merrill G Burlingame Special Collections)

PRESS NOTICES.

"Crossing the Plains in 1865," is the title under which a lady in the *Rocky Mountain Husbandman*, is publishing a series of letters. The story of every-day life on the plains is so prettily written, that these papers repay perusal. We have been charmed by the native grace of the author, and we send her our compliments whoever she may be. We crossed the plains the same year, also, six years before, and we can fully appreciate the experience of our unknown friend who writes so charmingly.—*Stock, Farm and Home Weekly.*

In this issue we close our narrative of pleasure, trials, etc., of a trip across the great American plains in 1865. It has been a plain, simple story and true to life and full of interest to Montana's oldtimers, and all who made the journey of the plains in wagons. To the editor of this paper it has been a story of particular interest, for he, a beardless boy then, crossed the plains, was a member of the McMahan train, the sick man for whom Dr. Howard often went foraging for bread.—*Rocky Mountain Husbandman.*

"Crossing the Plains in 1865," is the title of a story which was written by a well-known lady of Virginia City, for the *Rocky Mountain Husbandman*, and came to a conclusion in the last number of that paper.

It was a plain, unvarnished recital of the experiences of the journey across the plains when ox-trains were the favorite conveyances, and the voyagers were subjected to many vicissitudes unknown to travelers of the present day. Though quite unpretentious as to literary merit, it has been interesting in recalling to the minds of the pioneers, who have read it, the eventful scenes of their own pilgrimage, and to them, it has been pleasant reading.—*Madisonian.*

"I have felt a deep interest in S. R. H.'s, 'Crossing the Plains in 1865,' all through these long series of letters, and many a familiar spot has been brought back to me that had long been forgotten. And as some of the actors in the play live in Challis, I will say to S. R. H., that Mrs. Hardinbrooke is still loved by a large circle of friends, and that little Annie is now a blooming young lady, and ever worthy the good-bye kiss; that the Captain has never disgraced the title bestowed in 1865.

"I am, Mr. Editor, respectfully yours,

"O. E. PENWELL."

I hope you have enjoyed this exciting set of stories! These diaries and biographies make American history come alive in a way no novel or secondhand tale can do.

Be sure to collect the other books in the Knowledge Keepers Home Library Series, and help preserve our history in print for generations to come! Many of these books now include free study guides for teaching history, available to download at KnowledgeKeepersBookstore.com

TRUE STORIES of
NEBRASKA PIONEERS

NEBRASKA SOCIETY OF THE
DAUGHTERS OF THE
AMERICAN REVOLUTION

1844   *Knowledge* KEEPERS
HOME LIBRARY SERIES

Diary of a New York Girl

Caroline Richards Clarke

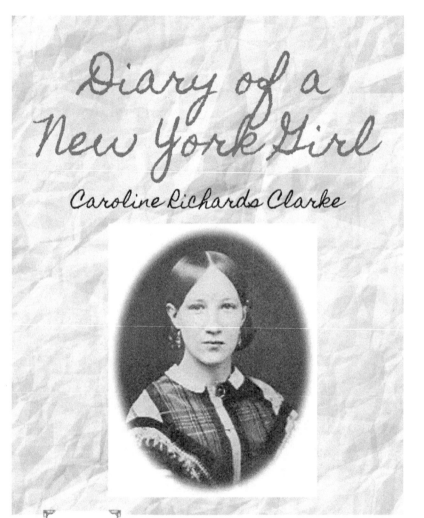

1852   KnowledgeKEEPERS
HOME LIBRARY SERIES

UP THE WESTERN TRAIL
THE LOG OF A COWBOY
BY ANDY ADAMS

WITH MAPS AND PHOTOGRAPHS

1872 *Knowledge* KEEPERS
HOME LIBRARY SERIES

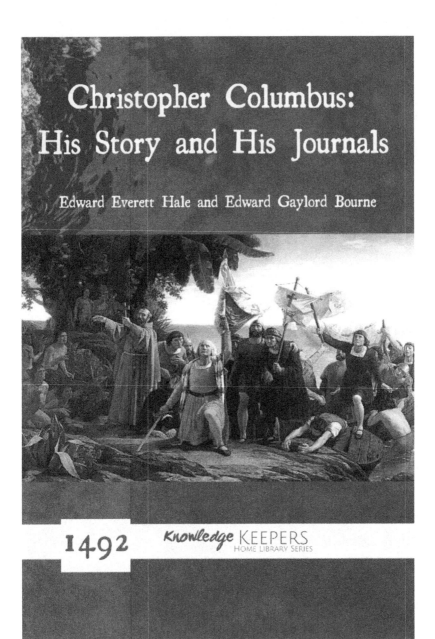

Christopher Columbus:
His Story and His Journals

Edward Everett Hale and Edward Gaylord Bourne

1492   *Knowledge* KEEPERS
HOME LIBRARY SERIES

GENERAL LEE
Southern Commander

A Life of General Robert E. Lee
and
Recollections and Letters of Robert E. Lee

1861   *Knowledge* KEEPERS
HOME LIBRARY SERIES

ABLE AND

MIGHTY MEN

BIOGRAPHIES OF THE MEN WHO SIGNED
THE DECLARATION OF INDEPENDENCE

By L. Carroll Judson

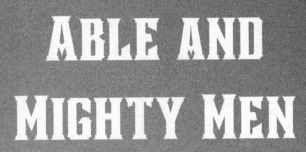

1776   *Knowledge* KEEPERS
HOME LIBRARY SERIES

MILES STANDISH
THE PURITAN CAPTAIN

BY JOHN S. C. ABBOTT

1620　*Knowledge* KEEPERS
HOME LIBRARY SERIES

IROQUOIS HANDBOOK

HISTORY, MANNERS, AND CUSTOMS OF THE INDIAN NATIONS WHO ONCE INHABITED PENNSYLVANIA AND THE NEIGHBOURING STATES

BY THE REV. JOHN HECKEWELDER

1771   *Knowledge* KEEPERS
HOME LIBRARY SERIES

Made in the USA
Monee, IL
04 May 2023

32973868R00154